THE MAGIC AND WISDOM

OF THE BIG CATS

By

Cindie Ambar with Cathy O'Brien

Table of Contents

Dedication

To all the animals who chose to incarnate on Earth, and all they sacrificed to save the human race.

Acknowledgments

To my father, from whom my deep love of animals came.

To my beloved husband, Todd, who has supported me in all my endeavors and whose love and belief in me keep me grounded and inspired.

To my cats, Pookie and Althea, who taught me to be truly present, enhancing my connection to animals, my healing abilities, and my life in so many ways.

To all the animals I have loved and worked with, for everything you have taught me and for the beauty and magic you have brought into my everyday existence.

To Kathleen Prasad and her Let Animals Lead method of Reiki, whose principles I apply to every aspect of my work with animals.

To Tamra Oviatt and Rochelle Stanley, who supported me in releasing my self-imposed blocks and limitations and made this work possible.

To Andi Rive, David, and Ansa Gerber your love and dedication to these sacred beings is magnificent, and your willingness to trust Cathy and me to support them is deeply appreciated.

To Cathy O'Brien, who has been my partner in this work for close to 15 years. Your dedication to the animals of this planet is magnificent and beautiful, and your energy is present on every single page of this book. While I may have technically "written" the book, this publication reflects our joint commitment to and work with these magnificent, sacred beings.

About the Author

Cindie Ambar's life purpose is to bring joy, healing, and transformation to humans and animals alike. She left a high-paying job in Silicon Valley to pursue her life's work. As a healer, animal communicator, and mystic, she draws on her direct experience to share insights into the hearts and minds of the big cats at two South African sanctuaries. Their stories are moving, and their wisdom is profound.

Introduction

All life is sacred. Every non-human living being deserves our love, respect, and our support. When you live in connection with the natural world and its beings, magic will fill your life and heal your hearts, as it has ours. It is the most beautiful and profound way to change the world.

The purpose of this book is to bring attention to both the challenges that big cats face all over the world and their profound spiritual beauty and importance to mankind. Not only are a number of species dealing with extreme habitat loss, many are nearing extinction. Big cats are held in captivity in horrific conditions in many parts of the world, abandoned and left to die or fend for themselves in war zones, housed in "canned hunting" facilities in which they are trapped and shot at close range, inbred for profit to their own detriment, poisoned and killed to harvest their body parts, and much more. Until the practice was banned fairly recently, in the United States you could literally buy a lion or tiger cub at the side of the road. Private ownership of these beautiful beings still exists.

My partner, Cathy O'Brien, and I have had a close connection with big cats for almost 15 years that we have been partnering together, and in particular, for the four years we have actively been supporting cats in two South African sanctuaries with healing and animal communication. They have taught us so much, and we are beyond honored to be called their friends, to be considered one of them. They are magnificent and must be protected, as should all animals, so they can complete their healing work on the planet. We owe them so much more than you can possibly imagine. I am including a chapter to let you know how you can help.

In February of 2025, one of our cats informed us it was time to take our work to a larger scale. Another shared with us: "Your book will change the lives of many. It is critical that you focus on this task until it is complete. There are lions' lives that depend on it. It is more than a book; it is a revolution. God bless you for leading the charge and doing so with so much love. More will be revealed soon."

The cats asked us to write this book, and they need you. YOU have the power to make a difference.

My Story

I **live in the same coastal community I was born in.** I was blessed to grow up with a large, extended Italian family. My dearest friends are my sisters. I also spent close to every other weekend growing up with my first cousins, Candy and Lisa. My parents loved animals, and I grew up with three dogs and multiple cats. My father was someone who would be referred to as a "man's man," and the only times I saw him cry as a child were over the injury to or loss of our beloved family pets.

The Hole in My Heart

I had a difficult childhood. I did not get along with my parents and was labeled with an "attitude" problem. I never understood what my parents meant by that until later in life. My behavior was a legitimate concern in their eyes. However, at the time, I decided there was something wrong with me because I absolutely could not figure out what I was doing wrong. My parents did love me, but the attitude label left me feeling unloved and unwanted. I felt like an outsider at times, and misunderstood most of the time.

The attitude label left its mark on me, and I spent many years of my life trying to fill the hole in my heart. I would pray and pray to do better as a child, but I couldn't seem to shake it. I had overwhelming anxiety much of the time. I would try so hard to be good, just to be told I had an attitude problem over and over again. I became a perfectionist in an attempt to be accepted. If I didn't do anything wrong, how could anyone be angry with me? Perfection became a safety net.

This hole in my heart affected everything I did. I married young and loved my first husband, Joe, dearly. I was loving and affectionate with him but wasn't truly present. I was too busy trying to be perfect. I had straight A's as an undergraduate, with several A+ grades. I studied so much and so hard that I could literally mentally flip through my notes in my mind when taking a midterm. In graduate school, I realized I could study less and still do well, and I gave myself a small break from my unrealistic, self-imposed workload.

When I graduated and started working, I would often stay late and go in on weekends. After 13 years together, Joe was done. Looking back, I'm surprised he hung in there for so long.

Music and Spirituality

When I was eight years old, we were tested for musical ability at my elementary school. I showed promise, based on my scores, and chose the viola as my instrument. Through my viola, I learned what joy was and became connected with the magic life can hold. There was a feeling that came over me when I played an energy, a passion, and an overwhelming, intense feeling of love and peace. I devoted myself to my instrument.

My junior high school music teacher told the orchestra that I was "on fire." I excelled and was chosen to tour Europe with America's Youth in Concert, an orchestra composed of high school students from all over the country. I don't know that I was technically as talented as some others, but my passion and exuberance made people want to listen to me play. We performed at Carnegie Hall and the most famous concert halls in Europe. I loved the Italian audiences the best their exuberance and deep love of music was uplifting.

I loved going to church as a child. A number of the masses were in Latin, and I didn't understand most of what was being said in English, but I could feel the energy and reverence in the building. There was something special I felt there, although I didn't understand why. I was connecting with spiritual energy, and it felt mysterious and heart-opening.

I was raised Catholic, but I consider myself spiritual rather than religious. My primary use of prayer as a child started one day after eating at Kentucky Fried Chicken. I was terrified of vomiting, and at one point was saying close to 100 "Our Father" and "Hail Mary" prayers at night in exchange for settling my stomach! To this day, my Creator supports and guides me in my work.

When I was 18 years old, I did something I was deeply ashamed of. I couldn't stop thinking about it and was tormenting myself on a daily basis. Insomnia set in. One evening, in the middle of the night, lying sleepless in bed, I saw a beautiful soft golden light. Jesus came into my room and simply held me. It felt like a dream. It was a love so deep and profound something I had never experienced before. I began to heal almost immediately. I went back to church for several weeks, but it just wasn't for me.

My Connection to Animals

My passion for supporting and defending animals came early. We moved when I was in third grade. We lived close to a freeway exit, with a huge field next to us, and people often dumped animals on our property. We took in several feral cats. One extremely wet year, I heard faint sounds underneath my dad's shop on the property. Exploring further, I found a bedraggled, teeny kitten soaked and covered in mud. There were several others, and their mother. It was freezing, and there was so much water that it looked like an underground pond.

My heart broke for those little beings, and I felt angry as well. Who would do something like that? Why weren't their people making sure they were safe and dry? Our family cared for them and found homes. One, LC, became a family cat. He loved to ride in the car, and we took him camping once! From that day forward, every time it rained, I worried about the animals that were cold and hungry. This continued until I was in my late 20s. I felt tormented frequently in cold weather and helpless to do anything about it.

When I was in high school and my parents divorced, my mom bought a house within walking distance of our local animal shelter. My sister Debbie and I walked down three or four times a week. We prayed for the animals, sent them as much love as we knew how, and made plans to buy a farm and break all the animals out of the shelter to live there. We kept this up until my mother asked me to leave shortly after I turned 18.

Moving Forward

My mother's decision created another huge hole in my heart. She never explained what was going on just that I wasn't helping her enough. I was told to ask my dad if I could stay with him. I called, and when my stepmother answered, she said she would have to talk to him about it. I was panicked and afraid I would have nowhere to go.

My dad called soon after and invited me to stay. He was very kind, gentle, and loving. I am grateful for being asked to leave to this day. Healing took place in my father's house, and I began to understand who my father really was and how much he cared for me.

My mother and I had some rocky times until I was a bit older, but we have been dear friends ever since.

My Interest in Health and Healing

I was an avid reader as a young person. It helped me escape from my thoughts and feelings. I spent hours and hours cooped up in my room as a child. It was a challenge to find enough reading material. My mom would take me to the library, and I would read all the books we checked out in just a few days.

In elementary school, I began perusing my maternal grandmother's bookshelf. I was drawn to and read her health-related books. They were quite old at that time, written in the 1930s and '40s. I was fascinated. Of particular interest to me was any mention of tuberculosis. I had read a book about Helen Keller's teacher, who had died of tuberculosis, and became convinced that I had it.

Hypochondria was another major aspect of my childhood. I thought I had stomach cancer, but it was probably an ulcer from my constant worrying. In fifth grade, I had severe stomach pain and bloating one night after dinner. I remembered that I had been fighting on the monkey bars that day with a kid named Ruben. We had wrapped our legs around each other to try and pull each other down, as all the kids did on the bars.

I wasn't totally sure how babies were made but was beginning to think I might be pregnant. When the bloating subsided the next day, it was an enormous relief.

I had many instances in which I freaked myself out, thinking I had one disease or another. It provided some relief, taking the focus off of my other issues.

When I was seven, I began to watch a show called *Julia*. It was about a nurse. I loved the show and decided to be a nurse when I was older. I wanted to learn everything I could and started to "practice" with my sisters.

I had my youngest sister, Debbie, scrape her arm up on the pavement so I could heal her (I know, I know). I had been given a set of multiple tiny perfumes for Christmas. I mixed and matched from the bottles and used my healing concoction on her sore. I placed a big bandage over it. The next day, when I removed the bandage, the sore had disappeared. All three of us gasped at the discovery, and I was convinced that I had what it took to be a nurse. Little did we know at the time that the alcohol in the perfumes I mixed together simply dried the area out.

My "Nursing" Career

It wasn't until 40 years later that I realized what I had always wanted to be was a healer. But nursing was the only profession I knew that was available to me as a child in the '60s.

When I graduated from high school, I took pre-nursing classes at my local community college. I was fascinated by and loved every single one of them, although Organic Chemistry was my least favorite. I completed my prerequisites and applied to the school's nursing program. It was impacted, so I enrolled in a certified nurse's assistant program to make myself more competitive.

I trained in a nursing home, and I didn't enjoy it. On my last day, an unbelievable number of unpleasant and strange things happened. When I looked back on it, some of my "adventures" were absolutely hilarious. It blessed me with the best English paper I had ever written, but it should have been my first signal from the universe that nursing was not for me.

I had planned to be a nurse my whole life and was determined. Nothing was going to stop me. When I began the formal nursing program, I loved the coursework but feared and disliked the clinical practice. They placed us first in a nursing home, which was the kiss of death for a number of my classmates. I plodded on but became more and more uneasy. Nursing was not what I thought it was going to be. I was gaining some incredible knowledge but began to understand that using it was the realm of physicians in those days. I would be performing primarily supportive functions.

A Change of Plans

I began to think that what I really wanted to be was a physician. I was also dreading my hospital rotation. And I don't know that I was cut out for either medical role. The thought of giving the wrong medication or making a decision that negatively impacted a patient scared the hell out of me.

I had known in my heart since starting the program that it wasn't for me, but I forced myself onward because my whole life had been focused on achieving this goal. Now I had to come to terms with it. It was an agonizing decision. My entire family was extremely disappointed in me, with the exception of my paternal grandmother. I left the program and felt a freedom I had not known in a very long time.

I was absolutely lost for a number of months. The depression and anxiety were overwhelming. My intention had never been to work in a hospital or office, but to be a Public Health Nurse. After some searching, I enrolled in a bachelor's program for health services professionals that had its emphasis in public health. I was back to what I loved. I was particularly enamored with my epidemiology class.

Epidemiology is about the distribution and determinants of disease, and ultimately, communicable disease and outbreak control. That fascinated me. When I graduated, I realized that without a nurse's license, I would need an advanced degree to do what I wanted to do. I enrolled in a master's program focused on public administration with a health policy focus, and I loved it.

Before I graduated, I was offered a public health job. I worked in the then-called "AIDS" program just as folks were becoming very aware and frightened. I then moved to the communicable disease program and loved that even more. My life goal of working for the Public Health Department had been achieved!

I developed an expertise in tuberculosis and eventually became the program coordinator. I absolutely loved my job and the idea of protecting the public from my old nemesis: *Mycobacterium tuberculosis.*

I did not have a nursing degree, but I developed a reputation for being an expert. I even had physicians call me for input but had to be careful to quote from established recommendations. I became faculty and a consultant at the National Tuberculosis Center in San Francisco. I was in love with fighting tuberculosis and enjoying my job immensely.

A New Direction

I was offered a job as the Tuberculosis Program Manager for the Santa Clara County Public Health Department, which was substantially larger than the department in Santa Cruz. A year and a half later, the county was dealing with enormous budget cuts.

As the last manager hired, it didn't matter what my skills or qualifications were. I would be the first to go. Public service rules.

Another manager and I were sent to interview with the Director of Social Services. The hope was that the other manager would be chosen for his opening and they could keep me in Public Health.

When I interviewed and the director, Will Lightbourne, spoke about his vision, I was inspired. Instead of remaining fearful about what would happen to me, I became excited about a new future. He chose me.

I spent happy years writing grants and developing and implementing programs to support children and families in the child welfare system. Will was an amazing collaborator. He was open to all of my ideas, and I was assigned to a number of exciting projects.

The opportunity to work in child welfare and support children as well as families was an amazing one, and very healing for me, given my childhood experiences. Unfortunately, after 11 years, Will took a job as the Director of the California Department of Social Services.

For over a decade, I had worked for the Agency Director as his emissary to support child welfare. In his absence, I transferred there. While the Child Welfare Director adored me, it was a bit of a rude awakening. I was no longer insulated by my status as a direct report to the Social Services Agency Director.

The department had a long history of problems, exacerbated by the former Child Welfare Director, who had instilled fear throughout the entire agency and treated everyone, including her managers, atrociously.

The Beginning of the End

My first day was December 26. It was the slowest time of the year, and I was excited about the opportunity to read and review agency policies and manuals and to start to get a leg up on my new role.

I had a wonderful first morning, but after lunch, I was approached by one of my new staff members. She reported that another staff member was smoking pot in the parking lot. It went downhill from there and continued to get worse.

We had many amazing managers and social workers who excelled at what they did, truly loved their work, and cared about their families. But relationships between social workers and managers, and between line staff and managers, were atrocious. Relationships among individual staff were strained as well.

It was an almost surreal dog-eat-dog experience. Daily backstabbings, mini-coup attempts, and outrageous fights among line staff, supervisors, and managers were rampant. People lied effortlessly to get back at others. It was truly the nastiest place I could ever imagine working for. And it was a highly successful department that got results.

It soon began to take its toll on me. I was warned by several people that I would become ill if I continued working there. The high pressure and highly visible nature of my work, long hours, and daily commute were just the tip of the iceberg.

The Healing Journey Begins

Several years before, I had begun my healing journey, and while working for Will, I had been assigned to an enormous project as the Project Director of our Family Wellness Court for Infants and Toddlers. My long hours expanded, and my freedom was more limited. I was working with multiple county department directors and child welfare judges who had difficulty finding time to meet. I spent a number of very late Friday nights at the office.

While on vacation, I suffered a concussion, and it was several months before I was able to work full time again. A friend had referred me to an energy healer, who I attribute my healing to. She identified the challenge as a neck issue rather than an unresolved concussion, and I felt better immediately.

Anana believed that I had a gift and began to train me. I was trained in Theta Healing as my first modality. I wasn't interested in Reiki, but when my Theta Healing instructor told us it would make us animal and child magnets, I was all in.

Soon after my training was complete, I learned about animal Reiki and began to study with Kathleen Prasad, the founder of animal Reiki, as well as the Shelter Animal Reiki Association (SARA), whose members volunteer weekly in shelters and sanctuaries.

I wanted to volunteer with the dogs at my local animal shelter, but they were not ready to embrace alternative forms of healing. Kathleen's SARA co-founder, Leah D'Ambrosio, was on the board of a local horse sanctuary and suggested I check it out.

This visit was life-changing. I had always loved and wanted a horse when I was young, but we could only afford to go riding a couple of times a year at a local stable. I had lost my interest over time and had been focused on dogs and cats. I volunteered walking the dogs at the local shelter.

That day at Pregnant Mare Rescue, I made an immediate connection with a horse named Dually. My heart opened in a way I never realized was possible, and the next day, I could barely force myself to go to work. I felt a strong, magnetic energy pulling me back there, with Dually in particular. I began to volunteer Reiki once a week.

The horses loved it. They became very relaxed, and over time, it even supported the more fearful horses to begin to trust and feel safe.

Life-Changing Events

Things continued to devolve at my job. It was very difficult to force myself to go to work, but my high salary was needed as we had just purchased a new home. We had a new director, and it was time to develop and submit our budget proposal to the Board of Supervisors, which was my responsibility.

I had always been given everything I needed for the budget at the last minute and had to pull everything together with very little time. I always missed the manager's Christmas breakfast because I was racing the clock.

This year was much worse. Our new director needed time to assess the budget before we planned and submitted a new one. While I had always been able to turn everything around with lightning speed, I was having trouble concentrating.

The next day, my husband was very unexpectedly laid off from his marketing job that he had held for 12 years. We had very little in the way of savings. I was shocked and stunned, and it exacerbated my inability to concentrate further.

I tried to go back to work on the budget time after time, but I could barely pull my thoughts together. With the deadline looming and everything else crashing around me, I simply could not do it. I became terrified and panicked. I couldn't sleep, didn't want to eat, and my muscles were so tight that it was difficult to move my body.

Depression began to set in, and it was mentally impossible to continue to work on the budget. Within a couple of days, it had become impossible for me to concentrate on anything at all. I was unable to perform my job and was just going through the motions.

The pressure I had been under all those years, and the added stress of my husband being unemployed, broke me.

I had a medical note that granted me a leave of absence, but later I decided I couldn't return to work. My husband asked me if I could stay, for just a while. It broke my heart to tell him I couldn't. At a time when he needed me the most, I "retired" from my job. I was in a deep depression and refused to take medication. I lost interest in absolutely everything and felt almost no feelings at all, except depression and terror.

I did nothing but sit on the couch. After a while, I stopped bathing, and I was not eating. My beloved husband did everything he could to get me to eat, but I tossed out almost everything he took the time to lovingly prepare for me. Every hour, every minute felt like an eternity. I slept for a grand total of two interrupted hours per night, if that. At times, I didn't sleep at all.

I became incredibly weak, and when I did decide to bathe, my husband had to help me from start to finish. He was panicked and extremely worried about me, as I refused to see anyone, including my beloved family. For months, I left the house only for the rare doctor's appointment. The endless days dragged on. I wanted to die and started to look into methods to release myself from my misery.

My husband was frantic and let my doctor know what was going on. I went in for a visit, and she let me know that she had notified the authorities. As I was leaving the office building, I could see sheriff's deputies outside waiting for me. I ran and evaded them for about fifteen minutes, then gave in. I was placed in the back of a patrol car and taken to a local mental health facility a locked facility.

The Healing Begins

This was absolutely the best medicine for me. I hated it, but I got on medication and began to feel human again. The place was horrific, with other patients coming into my room at night, things being stolen from me, men and women placed in adjacent rooms, and highly psychotic patients in the same space as those with depression. There was screaming night and day.

I was in for a month, out for several weeks, and then back in again for another several weeks. I had started to go downhill when I was released, and thankfully was placed in an excellent facility with care that was meaningful and without being overmedicated. I was released on the third of July. It was the strangest Fourth ever, but at least I was free. Independence Day had a whole new meaning for me.

Over my last several years of work, I had begun to train in additional healing modalities and animal communication. Bureaucrat by day and healer on nights and weekends. I had taken on volunteer communication and healing work with an additional horse sanctuary. There were ostriches, emus, mini-donkeys, goats, sheep, and more. It was there that I met the greatest animal loves of my life four horses who have traveled with me from lifetime to lifetime, although I wasn't aware of it at the time.

It was a magical experience and so much fun to experience healing and communication with so many other species.

It took some time to recover from the depression completely. I got a part-time mental health job, continued to train in various healing methods, and began to establish a practice. Two years later, I had enough income to quit my job and live my life as a full-time healer and animal communicator. Life was beautiful again.

My New and Exciting Life

My business began to grow, and I was ecstatic. I could not believe I was being paid to do something I loved so deeply and that gave me so much joy. I fell in love with every animal I worked with and had amazing human clients as well. I looked forward to each and every day.

My experience with animal communication confirmed for me what I have always known: animals are divine beings with profound wisdom to share, and they are here to heal their people and the planet. All of their personalities were vastly different, and I had some hilarious, as well as moving and inspirational, conversations.

One dog called the new dog in the household an "attention-grabbing little whore." Others cracked hilarious jokes, while still others shared their deep wisdom and understanding with their human companions. They knew exactly what their humans needed, whether it was to begin a meditation practice or work on loving themselves. One dog even suggested that her person needed to "get laid."

As a communicator, I can tell you there is absolutely no difference between species when it comes to intelligence. I have had as profound a conversation with a housefly as with a horse. More on that later!

I worked with animals of all kinds all over the world, and more horses and dogs than any other animal. I had magical and life-changing experiences on a daily basis. I also communicated with and supported the wildlife around my home.

A number of years into the communication and healing work, I began to feel an urge to make an impact on a broader scale. That is the subject of this book.

About Animals

Who Are Animals?

It's important to begin with an understanding of who animals are and their purpose here on Earth. Animals are sacred, sentient beings. By "animal," our definition includes all non-human living things that are not part of the plant kingdom. We consider insects to be animals as well. They share similar characteristics and gifts, although they do not have the same connection to humans as non-insect beings, due to centuries of conflict with humans.

Animals have their own life purpose and contribute to and support their humans in actualizing their life purpose. They have tremendous wisdom and understand everything that is going on in the world, as well as everything that is going on in their people's lives. Animals have a global consciousness. When COVID was plaguing the Earth, the animals communicated their insights about current events and everything that their people were struggling with.

The day the Israel–Hamas conflict began, one of my teachers, who sings to the whales, observed a great deal of distress being communicated through their songs.

Roles Animals Play in Our Lives

The following statement from a horse about her person illustrates the critical role that animals play in our lives. This horse was much less interested in conversing about herself than in helping her person understand their true purpose together and in helping that person realize her true purpose in the world.

The conversation began with, "I am here to talk about K, primarily. Then we can talk about other things. I want her to love herself and take better care of herself. There is part of her that doesn't love herself or appreciate her inner beauty. She has far to go in this human experience, and I would like you to help her by your healing energy and magic. She needs her special light to shine and grow so she can help the horses, but she hides this light under a bushel, you might say.

You must realize that K is special and that our relationship is a very special and deep one. We have been meant to be together for eons. She has a very special role on this planet in this lifetime. She must be supported so that we equines can flourish and grow under her care and supervision. I have done so. She has transformed my life from one of hell to one of beauty and love. She is on a journey that will change the lives of horses everywhere. That is why I have chosen her. I am an emissary from all horses to this sacred being, and I am here to support and contribute to her growth."

In our conversations with animals, we frequently hear similar statements regarding their humans. Animals are also excellent advisors when it comes to helping their humans improve their lives.

They may suggest that their person work on loving themselves, recommend a specific activity, or even a career they know their person is suited for.

Animals and Intelligence

Animals have taken a subservient role on Earth by choice. They are here to love us, support us, and most importantly, to help us evolve. Animals are, by far, the most intelligent beings on our planet. Humans have an incredibly limited and anthropomorphic way of measuring intelligence. Most of what we measure regarding intelligence are skills, rather than innate intelligence or wisdom.

By these methods, pigs have been determined to have the intelligence of a third grader; however, what was assessed was only a limited aspect of what intelligence truly is. Animals have a deep understanding of our current reality, as well as what the future holds. And our emotional intelligence pales miserably in comparison.

The sensitivity of animals' senses supports their brilliance. They can see what we cannot see, hear what we cannot hear, and feel what we cannot or will not allow ourselves to be aware of feeling.

It's important to understand that there is no difference in intelligence among animal species. We have had as intelligent a conversation with a fly as we have with an elephant. There is a beautiful book, considered to be the first treatise on animal communication, written in the 1940s, entitled *Communication With All Life*. In this book, the author develops a deep and meaningful relationship with a famous dog but also spends a month in relationship with a housefly, from whom he learned a considerable amount.

I had an enlightening experience with a fly a number of years ago, early in my animal communication studies. A fly landed on my bare skin, and I asked it to please move onto a piece of my clothing. When the fly asked why, I related that I had heard that flies vomit when they land. The fly was both insulted and disgusted. He explained, in great detail, what the world would be like without flies. He persisted until I got the picture and apologized.

Animals as Healers

Animals are healers, as well as our teachers. Animal communicators and healers often come away from a session "for" an animal, only to realize that a headache has disappeared, their stomach has settled, or their depression or frustration has transformed into feelings of love or peace. This has been a common occurrence for myself, as well as my colleagues.

When I go whale watching, I always come away with the feeling of having been healed in some way, and my heart feels incredibly open. Whenever I go to see my heart horses in Northern California, I feel the same.

It's helpful to understand that our animals are our mirrors. It's not uncommon for animals to have the same physical or emotional challenges as their people, and I have seen quite a bit of this in my practice. While it is true that animals sometimes take on the issues of their humans in an attempt to heal them, I find more commonly that animals are drawn to humans who share some of the challenges they themselves need to work through in a given lifetime.

It's important to understand that animals will also sometimes take charge when their person is unable or unwilling to protect themselves. They can act out our feelings as well. If you are suppressing feelings like anger, your dog or cat may very well snarl or growl at someone you know whom you may be suppressing feelings toward. If you are not feeling safe, your animal may very well be overprotective because they are picking up the need for safety from you.

Every once in a while, we have an animal tell us that they developed an issue so their person would get help, and occasionally, we have worked with animals who won't heal until we work with their person. Additionally, animals may exhibit what seem to be behavioral issues because they are in pain. There is a complete and total lack of understanding about this by many in the horse world, who unfairly blame their horses for their challenges.

What Your Animals Know About You

It's important to understand what your animals know about you. Absolutely everything! There is nowhere to run, nowhere to hide. They know everything that you are saying and everything that you are thinking, no matter how far away from home you are.

There is a barn near my house where the animals were not being well taken care of. I used to call out to them every day when I passed by, telling them how beautiful and sacred they were. One day, seemingly out of nowhere, I heard the statement, "Pookie told me about this!" My cat, Pookie, had been a bit uneasy about my relationship with and love for horses. Apparently, she had been warning my newly adopted cat about this! Two miles away from Cindie's home, Althea knew exactly what I was doing and did not approve!

An animal communication mentor of Cindie's related a story in training about a cat that started urinating on every item of her client's husband's clothing. They were really puzzled by the behavior until she revealed in a communication session that she was upset because she knew the husband was having an affair and she could smell the other woman on the husband's clothes. When her mentor informed her human client about this, the woman said she already had her suspicions and now they were confirmed.

In short, never underestimate an animal. It's unfortunate that so many do.

About Animal Communication

The intention of this chapter is to provide some basic information about animal communication. There are many excellent books written on the subject, with Penelope Smith being my favorite. I have also studied with a number of instructors I highly recommend, including Penelope Smith, Nedda Wittel, Sandy Rakowitz, and Thea Strom. While books can be incredibly helpful, it is highly recommended to study with a seasoned communicator as well. There are ethical considerations to be aware of, ways to conduct a session to obtain the best and most accurate information, and delicate issues that require a special approach. It is also incredibly helpful in terms of addressing behavioral issues, which can be challenging and may require energy healing support and/or work with a trainer in addition to communication to resolve.

Who Can Communicate with Animals?

Communicating with animals does not require any special "gift." Every single human being is capable of communicating with animals, and many of us did so easily and effortlessly as children. I came to animal communication later in life. I began to spontaneously receive messages after I became an animal Reiki practitioner. The first messages were simple and often involved animals who were not fond of their names.

What Is Animal Communication?

Animal communication, at its most basic, is a telepathic connection and exchange of information between a human and a non-human being. Animals communicate among themselves telepathically, via pheromones, and by using specific signals and behaviors. It is possible to communicate with every animal species, including insects and even plants. Animal communicators also frequently speak with animals who have crossed over.

How Do Animal Communicators Receive Messages?

Animal communicators receive information in multiple forms. Some, like myself, hear the animals' words. Presumably, animals do not speak in full sentences, but this is the way I receive messages. Communicators may see images or videos that tell a story, smell something related to the animal, taste something relevant to the communication session, and many have a "knowing" they just understand what is going on and what the animal would like to communicate. Most of us also feel what is going on in the animal's body, which can be very helpful since animals tend to underplay illness.

One other form of receiving is through touch. In my first animal communication class, we were given bundles of fur and asked to relay a message from the animal connected to that fur. Mine was tan, a bit wavy, and clearly belonging to a dog, but when I touched the fur, I got an image of an orange cat twitching his tail, obviously hunting and looking as if he was just about to pounce on something.

I was horrified. How could I be so wrong? I listened to the others who shared their messages before me and was embarrassed to share mine. When I did, our instructor laughed and let me know that the fur was from her dog, Merlin, who had just been punished for killing rabbits in the barn. This was his way of communicating that it was the neighbor's cat who was responsible!

Who Animal Communicators May Communicate With

It is possible not only to communicate with mammals, but also with animals of every species birds, lizards, and even insects. It is also possible to communicate with plants. And, because most communicators have psychic abilities, we can speak to animals who have crossed over as well as those here in physical form. Many communicators have advanced psychic abilities and can even communicate with crossed-over humans. While this is something I have done only rarely by request, crossed-over loved ones do come into my healing sessions to give advice or to relay beautiful and loving messages.

How to Support Yourself in Beginning a Practice

The most essential prerequisites to animal communication are the capacity to be fully grounded, in your body, and to have a receptive mind. Beginning a meditation practice is a wonderful way to start. It took me many years to be able to truly meditate, but when I learned to ground and center myself before engaging in meditation, everything shifted.

It is also important to recognize that it's almost impossible for a human being to have a completely still mind. Thoughts will continue to come in when you are meditating, but it's how you handle those thoughts that makes a difference. You simply notice them without engaging in them. If you suddenly remember you have to make dinner in 20 minutes, it's the difference between acknowledging and accepting the thought versus starting to plan your dinner menu. The best advice I have ever heard is to "let your thoughts pass like clouds."

Animal Intelligence and Personalities

Through my communication practice, it became clear to me that there is no difference not only in intelligence between humans and animals but among animal species. I have had as sophisticated a conversation with a fly as I have had with a whale. We measure intelligence in a very anthropomorphic way, and much of what we measure is learned.

Animals understand everything that is going on in the world and with their people, and they have an emotional intelligence that by far dwarfs that of humans. Animals also vary in their personalities. I have some very demure animal clients and those who swear like truck drivers. Some of my clients have a great sense of humor and make me laugh! They have strong and sound advice for their people. They may talk about a person needing to learn to love themselves, move in a specific career direction, identify and acknowledge a special gift, and on one occasion, even suggest that their human needed to "get laid"!

About Energy Healing

Overview

Energy healing is a holistic practice that includes healing for the mind, body, and spirit. It is distinguished from Western medicine by Western medicine's focus primarily on the physical body. The reality is that illness begins in the emotional body before it ever becomes a physical issue, and many of our challenges in life are related to unhealed trauma particularly childhood trauma.

Another primary distinction between Western medicine and energy healing is that energy healing can be performed from a distance. The cats are thousands of miles away, but we are able to share our healing energy regardless. Finally, while Western medicine is focused on ameliorating symptoms, energy work is focused on addressing root causes and restoring wholeness on every level.

There are many holistic practices that fall into this category. Reiki is one of the most common; however, between Cathy and me, we are trained in close to 25 different methods. We are both certified Dolphin~Whale healers, channeling the healing energy and wisdom of the Cetaceans, as well as being trained at the Reiki Master's level. We also have methods of our own.

One of my favorites is the Emotion Code/Body Code, developed by Dr. Bradley Nelson. It is incredibly helpful in pinpointing the root causes of physical, emotional, behavioral, and spiritual challenges. Additionally, past lives influence our experiences in our current lifetime. Clearing past lives can be incredibly powerful as well.

Beliefs are a powerful driving force behind both behavior and life outcomes in humans and animals. However, 94% of beliefs are subconscious. The beliefs we develop between the ages of 0 and 7 are some of the most critical in shaping our lives. At that age, most of us believe everything adults tell us and don't have filters such as, "Oh, Mommy is just having a bad day." Identifying and releasing those beliefs is a powerful way to create transformation and is a routine part of energy healing work.

Humans and animals also take on oaths, vows, and commitments that may have served them in one lifetime but no longer support them in the current one. Identifying and releasing these can help them get unstuck and move forward toward their goals.

Healing for Animals vs. Humans

Healing work with animals and humans is almost identical. Animals and humans are incredibly similar physiologically. They have the same internal organs, structures, and use the same processes. Just as importantly, both humans and animals may have past lives that require healing, have taken oaths and commitments that keep them stuck in some way, and hold limiting beliefs that may be released to support their healing (such as "All humans are bad").

Both Cathy and I are animal communicators. This is incredibly helpful in our work and supports our sanctuaries in understanding how the cats are feeling and what kind of support they may need. It also allows us to share beautiful messages from the cats with the humans who love them so deeply and are so devoted. It gives us the capacity to offer healing on the same level that we do for humans.

Who Can Facilitate Energy Healing

Every human being on the planet is capable of both animal communication and energy healing. It simply requires training, along with releasing limiting beliefs such as, "I am not intuitive." Animals can facilitate healings as well.

How We Heal

Many healers trained in multiple methods perform a more intuitive type of healing, drawing from various modalities and practices according to spiritual or personal guidance. That is how Cathy and I work together.

That said, the way we perform healing together has evolved. Most frequently, when working with a group, we do not always perform the work directly. We simply set our intention for healing, and we witness the energy beginning to flow, with creatures of all kinds coming in to support the beings we are working with. The results speak for themselves.

Consent and Letting Animals Lead

Central to the success of energy work is having the permission of the being you are working with. We use the Let Animals Lead approach in everything we do. With animals, both the animal's and their human's permission is required. The animal must always be in charge of the session. They always have choice. We move at their pace and do only what they wish us to do.

This is not only the most respectful way to approach healing but also the most effective. When you have the active participation of the being you are working with, the results can be amazing. Without it, no healing at all may occur.

Reiki and the Let Animals Lead Method

What Is Reiki?

Because I speak so frequently about Reiki in this book, I added a chapter to help deepen your understanding of what Reiki is. Reiki was first practiced in Japan, and the term literally translates to "spiritual energy" or "universal life force energy." It is a holistic modality that supports its recipients on multiple levels physical, emotional, spiritual, and behavioral.

Unlike many other healing methods that are based on using different techniques, processes, and practices, Reiki energy is shared between the practitioner and the recipient with one simple goal: whatever is the highest and best for the being we are working with. It is about being with, rather than doing something to or for a human or an animal. The energy is shared, and the recipient is able to use that information for their own healing.

When I Use Reiki

Although I may use Reiki at any time, I most commonly turn to Reiki when I am working with a group of animals, since the energy is capable of supporting multiple animals at once. It is also wonderful for developing a relationship and building trust with animals I am just getting to know or who have recently arrived at a sanctuary or shelter.

Most practitioners do a daily Reiki meditation and include multiple humans and animals. Reiki is also wonderful when you don't understand what is going on, because the energy is intelligent and will always go where it's needed. For one-on-one sessions, I tend to use methods that are more individualized and specific.

Reiki with Humans vs. Animals

Reiki with humans is more complex and typically involves several beautiful rituals, including specific hands-on healing positions, as well as different mantras and symbols. Reiki with animals is similar, and also quite different. It is not about doing to or for, but being with and simply sharing the healing energy.

While a human often needs hands-on contact to feel and connect with the energy, an animal almost always senses the energy and connects with it, if they wish. At some of the sanctuaries and other facilities that I support, I can feel the animals connecting, sometimes as soon as I am on my way.

Reiki is also equally effective from a long distance. However, some humans have difficulty feeling the energy that way. Not infrequently, the human is not as sensitive to the energy from a distance, while their animal is often extremely relaxed and deeply asleep.

How to Learn Reiki

I am extremely grateful to have been trained in the Let Animals Lead™ (LAL) method of Animal Reiki, as developed and taught by Kathleen Prasad of Animal Reiki Source. Kathleen is considered the godmother of Animal Reiki, and her approach is one that almost any animal will connect with. Other forms of Reiki are more intrusive, and animals are much less likely to be receptive to them.

In my opinion, having practiced and been trained in Reiki for almost 20 years, Kathleen's approach is the only way to go, and we highly recommend training with either Kathleen herself or one of her teachers. I have had multiple teachers and can speak with authority on this subject. Additionally, Kathleen's lineage is the Reiki Ryoho lineage, whose teachers go all the way back to the founder of Reiki himself, Mikao Usui.

What It Means to Let Animals Lead

The guiding principle behind the LAL method is that the animals are leading or in charge of the session and have choice. They can choose whether they want to participate in the Reiki and, if so, how they wish to receive the Reiki. Some animals love hands-on touch. Some do not.

The beautiful part of the LAL method is that Reiki can be done on any animal, anytime, anywhere whether or not you are in close proximity to them. As you can see in this book, Cathy and I regularly share Reiki with animals in South Africa while we are in California in the US.

How Is a Reiki Session Offered?

The approach is to "offer" Reiki to the beings you are working with and to create that peaceful space through breathwork and meditation. If they choose to participate, a beautiful heart connection can be felt by both the practitioner and the animal. This often leads to a powerful healing for both, and we could spend hours telling stories of our experiences sharing Reiki with different animals and the amazing results we have seen.

Again, Reiki can be offered to groups of humans or animals who can receive it at the same time, making it ideal to support larger animal groups. The other healing methods we use are offered one-on-one. With Reiki, we can share it with an entire herd of horses, all the animals at the zoo, a sanctuary, or another facility simultaneously.

Where to Learn Animal Reiki

If you are interested in learning more about the powerful healing of Animal Reiki, I encourage you to visit the website of our mentor and teacher, Kathleen Prasad of Animal Reiki Source: www.animalreikisource.com. You can study with Kathleen directly or learn from one of her teachers who will educate you in the LAL approach.

I am sure there are many other excellent teachers out there, but be sure to use the Let Animals Lead approach no matter who you study with. It means offering and being open to withdrawing if the animal is not interested, not touching the animal unless the animal clearly requests it, and keeping yourself at a distance of five to ten feet, allowing the animal to come closer only if they wish.

Our Journey With The Big Cats

CARE Foundation

Cathy and I met because of Reiki. We shared a Reiki instructor and began to get to know each other during a Reiki "share," in which students come together, learn new concepts, and practice their skills. At the time, I was creating a nonprofit for horses that focused on healing and animal communication. Cathy was interested and volunteered to support my efforts. We also both attended several Reiki events at Pregnant Mare Rescue, where I have been volunteering for the last 15 years.

It was during our Reiki Master's training at the CARE Foundation in Apopka, Florida, that we began to connect in a more meaningful way. Cathy, two other women, and I formed a close bond and spent time together before, during, and after the training.

It was a Siberian tiger named Balshoi who brought us more closely together. Balshoi was enormous, and if he didn't appreciate your presence, you could have several gallons of urine launched at you when you least expected it. Most of the class was a bit intimidated by Balshoi, but Cathy and I were not. We fell in love with him and spent a great deal of time with him.

You Are One of Us

After we returned, Cathy and I began to teach classes together. We also started visiting local zoos to bring peace and healing to the animals. It was difficult to see them under those circumstances, but we focused on bringing whatever comfort we could during our visits. We occasionally brought our Level 2 students with us.

We were always drawn to the big cats. More than ten years ago, we began to connect deeply with a lion and lioness at a local zoo. We felt an incredibly strong bond with them and spent a great deal of time with them on our trips. Not long afterward, they informed us that we were one of them. That explained a lot. We felt our connection with them deepen further with each visit. We were thrilled when their cub was born and saddened when the father passed away. Today, only their cub remains.

The Magic Begins

We had many magical experiences at the zoos and sanctuaries we frequented and came to know all the cats by name some by the names given to them, and others by their true names, which they shared with us. We worked with many species and supported a polar bear who rose out of a deep depression to become much more well-adjusted and content, along with many other animals who experienced incredible healings. It brought us tremendous joy to see the shifts in our beloved friends when we came to visit.

The way we approached the animals positively impacted other visitors. One day, several women with a group of very boisterous boys rushed through several exhibits before we arrived. The noise and chaos were taking a toll on the animals, and we spent much of our time calming them. We reached the snow leopards before the group and were sitting, deep in meditation, by the time they approached.

Instead of letting the boys run wild, one of the mothers began to shush them. Other visitors approached in a reverent, peaceful manner. The energy near the enclosure had shifted completely. There was a peace and stillness that had been lacking everywhere else in the zoo.

Inside the enclosure was a mother and several cubs. She got up, walked about twenty feet across the enclosure, and sat directly in front of us. There was only a quarter inch of glass between us. The group remained still, and we sat like that for close to twenty minutes. People came and went, but the silence prevailed.

The Work Deepens

We have four places we regularly visit and several others we visit occasionally. We've come to know many of the animals by name, and our relationships with them have developed and deepened over the years. We have shared healing energy with them, and they have shared their healing energy with us. They have taught us many things.

Now it is time to expand this work and make a difference for animals all over the planet.

The Guardians

The cats have recently shared more information about our role. Mela, a gorgeous lioness from Love Lions Alive, recently told us:

"You have a special role in this world. You have been appointed the guardians of the big cats not just us lions, but any other feline species walking the Earth. There is great joy among all of us, and great anticipation. This book will change things remarkably for us. It must be completed as quickly as possible. There are lions' lives that depend on it."

Our Pride

In February of this year, we began to receive information about our "pride" coming back together. One of the Isindile cats informed us it would be happening very soon, and several weeks later, two new cats arrived.

When we checked in with the pair, we felt tears of gratitude and overwhelming emotion. We sensed that we had shared past lives with these cats. No wonder our emotional response to them was so strong. The male said:

"We remember the time that we were together. The two of you were always the leaders. You were good leaders, just leaders, and we all thrived under your leadership. You have our undying, unconditional, and lifelong love and respect."

We had been reunited with our pride.

He also told us:

"It is time for you to step into your leadership role again."

He revealed that part of their reason for coming was to reconnect with us. Not long afterward, two new cats arrived at a sanctuary whose work we follow. The lioness shared the following message with us:

"Our pride is coming back together. This has been prophesied for many generations. You are indeed correct that the animals of the world will be taking their rightful place. You have had a key role a pivotal role in bringing this to pass. You are our true and magnificent leaders. Together, we will make this world a much better place."

The Beginning-Love Lions Alive

Cathy and I follow a number of zoo and sanctuary pages on Facebook regularly to support animals in need and to track their progress. She had discovered a big cat sanctuary that she was following called *Love Lions Alive (LLA)* and recommended that I check them out. I was immediately impressed by their website, Facebook page, and the energy of the cats, which felt content and peaceful to me despite the substantial trauma they had obviously experienced. I decided that I wanted to donate on a regular basis.

I tried to set up a recurring donation through PayPal; however, I was having difficulty sending the funds to South Africa. I messaged LLA and received instructions. I was guided to share with them that I was an animal communicator and healer and did pro bono work for sanctuaries and shelters. What did I have to lose? They were extremely interested and let me know they had just been discussing how helpful it would be to have people like us involved. I introduced them to Cathy, and there was a lot of excitement between the four of us about what was to come.

Our First Encounter

The first cats we were asked to support were a male and female Siberian tiger. They were called Igor and Kanosha. They had been kept as house pets and had arrived at LLA four days earlier. Andi explained that Igor was defensive and that they believed him to be depressed. Both cats had been in hiding, and she was concerned for their well-being.

We were given a list of questions for the cats and also information about all the love and care with which LLA developed their enclosures. The enclosure was in a forested area; they had created a pool for the tigers and had even chosen the individual rocks for the pool with great care. Andi wanted us to share the following with the cats:

"Please tell them that they are safe, they will get food always, we respect them and see them as awesome, majestic creatures. And we are honored to have the opportunity to get to know them."

It's important to note that just because a cat has been in the company of humans does not necessarily open them to trusting the human race. In fact, it can be quite the opposite. Many cats have had very negative experiences with "owners." In several parts of the world, big cats are acquired as status symbols, often enduring abusive circumstances. They don't appreciate being treated like objects and understand that they are being used by humans many of whom are ill-intentioned and almost all of whom have the cats with them for the wrong reasons.

All animals understand not only our words but also our thoughts and are highly emotionally intelligent. Many of these cats live in war zones and were left behind in their cages to face an excruciating fate. Even those that are rescued may have to endure shelling and bombing for months on end and are severely traumatized by the experience. It's important to understand that, even in the United States, any person could buy a lion or tiger cub at a roadside stand in a number of states until recently. This travesty has occurred on American soil as well.

Andi initially believed the "owners" had been good to Igor and Kanosha, but we came to find out otherwise as our relationship with them progressed. We did some healing work and communication with the tigers. They were greatly relieved to be told that they were in good hands but were still hesitant to fully believe that humans could be positive forces in their lives. We had no idea what kind of impact we had made and were anxious to find out.

The next day, we contacted Andi, who shared the following with us:

"I don't know what happened, but the tigers have changed like a switch was flipped. Like they woke up. They came out of the forest, they were calm and didn't try to hide. The female tiger, Kanosha, walked far out through the enclosure to the pool. A huge change."

We were ecstatic! We had the privilege of not only connecting with their beautiful, wise, sacred energy but also making a positive impact on their lives. We met on Tuesdays, which became our favorite day of the week!

We shared with Andi that we had a great conversation with both cats:

"They are awesome! They are a little overwhelmed from the transition, but they are very happy to be with you. They love you already and really appreciate all the thought and care you put into their area.

They did not want to talk about where they came from. They were very clear that they chose you, instead of the other way around. Igor was the only one who wanted to change his name. He feels 'Igor' has some negative connotations. He wanted us to make suggestions, and he chose 'Dakota.' It's a Native American name that means friend, ally.

They have amazing personalities! They are very spunky and fun-loving, but reminded us that it will take time for them to settle in so you can see who they are. In terms of what they need, they just need time to adjust and ask that you please be patient with their process. They love the space you created for them. They say that tigers are very secretive, don't show themselves a lot, and need places to hide which you have provided.

They would like to be reassured that they will remain with you for the rest of their lives. We told them, but they would like to hear it directly from you."

Andi let them know immediately.

We shared one more thing with LLA:

"They said you really see each animal as an individual, with individual personalities, needs, and wants. You appreciate each one as an individual."

This is not true with all humans, and they are very thankful to you for that.

Afterward, we received the following message:

"Thank you both for giving of yourselves. On Sunday, Cindie messaged us exactly as we were saying we wished we could talk to them."

Absolute synchronicity. This relationship was meant to be!

Cecil/Rasta

Our next task proved a bit more challenging. We were asked to communicate with a male lion named Cecil (now referred to as Rasta). It had literally taken years to rescue Cecil from Ukraine. The LLA website describes his circumstances perfectly:

"He had been living in dire conditions, in a barred cage, as an individual's 'object.' The Love Lions Alive team felt impassioned to take this lion out of his cage in the Ukraine and give him a South African home and a life of dignity and peace. People who had witnessed Cecil in the cage warned them that he was an 'abnormal' lion, because he banged his head into the bars of his cage repeatedly.

This, however, was in response to the life he was being forced to live at the time."

When Cecil arrived at LLA, he was not only severely traumatized but also quite physically ill. Several days later, we had the opportunity to connect with him.

We reported to Andi that we had just spoken with Cecil that morning.

"He is okay with his name. He really appreciates that you asked. He appreciates that you both realize the significance of a name and that you would show the care to make sure they are comfortable with their names. He feels that you are the first people who actually see him as an individual, and you have been using this name, and it feels good coming from you. He told Cindie, 'My name feels different coming from them.' So he is happy to keep that name."

"Cecil talked a lot about you and what it has meant to him to be with you. He said his heart has opened because of you. He said, 'My spirit is soaring with love and appreciation for all I have. I am blessed.' He really wanted us to tell you how happy he is to be with you. He feels that he is able to be himself here, to heal, and open his heart. He is getting better every day. You see his true nature and respect him as an individual. He has a lot of wisdom to share, and he knows you feel that. You 'see' him, and no human really has before. He is able to be his true self with you."

We also felt this might be a good time to share with Andi what our responsibilities and ethics are as animal communicators:

"It is our responsibility to take what the animal says and share with you what they want shared. They really appreciate the specific questions you are asking. And we have been taught that, to be respectful to the animal, we always begin any session by asking them what they would like to say. We always end every session by asking if there is anything else they want to say and clarify whether there is any information they would like to keep private. This helps develop openness and trust."

We continued to communicate with Cecil and share healing energy. He was polite and responsive, gentlemanly and formal in his manner of speaking. He shared that he was not that interested in speaking or interacting with humans.

As time went on, he began to ask us more questions and became very interested and curious about us. He began to enjoy our conversations, and we enjoyed him immensely. Our relationship has deepened remarkably, and we have had many fun adventures with this amazing cat!

Getting to Know More Cats

Our next assignment was to check in with the cats to see who wanted to come forward and speak or ask questions. We made sure the cats knew they could speak to us in confidence that they could trust us to share only what they gave their permission for.

It is an important aspect of animal communication to support the animal in speaking freely. If there is information we need to get across to ensure the animal's safety and well-being, we speak with them about how we can present the information without betraying their confidence but still inform their humans about the kind of support they need.

When we asked who wanted to come forward, it was Odin and Mulan a lion and lioness who were siblings and shared a space. Cecil asked if he could remain with us energetically. He did this to help the other cats feel safer, and they welcomed his presence. All the animals greatly respected him and already looked to him as a leader. His presence has been a blessing to everyone.

Their story from LLA is as follows:

"The Love Lions Alive team believes that Odin was born on the 7th of September, 2016, as he was four days old when we were called on the 11th of September to take him in. Odin was born on a lion breeding farm, where he had been intended to be a cub that tourists could bottle-feed and, eventually, be killed for the trade of lions' bones. However, Odin was a small, sickly, and dehydrated cub that the farm didn't believe was worth the money and effort to nurse back to health. Luckily for him, due to a tourist having the tenacity to find and reach out to us at Love Lions Alive, we had the opportunity to intervene. We collected him and his sister, Mulan, and bought the appropriate supplies from a veterinarian."

We reported back to Andi:

"There was some sort of recent change that they were feeling a little anxious about. We didn't get exactly what it was. They let us know that they wanted to be the most special to you and that they would like to be reminded frequently of that.

Mela and Carl came in, but they were nervous and stayed more on the periphery. Next time they may be more open. Cathy and I offered Reiki to all the cats, and they all participated. They loved the energy. I think it will take a bit for Mela and Carl to trust us, but we made some forward movement on that today."

We later found out that the "change" had been a small fire that destroyed much of the greenery in their enclosure and put them on edge.

Expanding our Connection with the Cats

We continued to connect with more of the cats and to learn more about their personalities and roles at LLA. Reign, a lioness, had a lot to say. She spoke of how powerful and magnificent she was. She informed us that she is taking part in the healing of the planet for all animals. She also said she holds down the energy of the sanctuary and keeps everyone grounded.

Demira, another lioness, referred to herself as the merrymaker of the group. She said she keeps the energy light and happy at LLA.

We also began to move into individual energy healing sessions, in addition to the Reiki we offered the group each time we connected. We began with Cecil, who had a number of physical issues related to malnutrition and inadequate care, but more importantly, he needed to release the trauma he suffered during his years of captivity. We were rewarded with a magnificent photo of him deeply at peace. Andi was astounded at how happy and relaxed he was. It was definitely a turning point.

We did the same for Igor and Kanosha.

We continued to get to know more LLA cats and connected with Shannon and Sienna, who lived with their sibling, Reign. They also expressed their knowledge and awareness of the plight of other big cats (and other animals) in South Africa and around the planet.

They informed us that many of the cats at LLA feel that they have a higher purpose to help other animals and it is not a coincidence that they all came together here to be with Andi. They want to bring healing to animals of all kinds and help shift the relationship between animals and humans on the planet.

Several of the cats had experienced even deeper trauma at the hands of the human race. Phuku, a lioness, had been born into the cub-petting industry and had been transferred to various locations over the course of her life.

The LLA description says:

"At the last location Phuku was at, poachers broke in and poisoned the other lions. They hacked off the lions' faces and paws. Phuku witnessed this massacre. She was extremely fortunate in that the male she was with had not been poisoned, so the poachers were too weary to go for her. The poachers would, however, likely come back. Phuku's owner contacted Love Lions Alive with the urgent situation. The poachers did return and tried to get her and the male she was with within the six weeks it took for the permit to be processed."

We discovered that Phuku suffered from survivor's guilt. She was also still incredibly traumatized by her experience. She explained to us that she would hear the men come in to dismember the cats they had killed and would try to be as still as possible to avoid being discovered.

We did quite a bit of healing work with her. In addition to the severe and long-lasting emotional trauma, she had multiple physical challenges from her experience. Phuku is an incredibly compassionate and magnanimous being, who loves to be called in to support other cats or animals in need.

Luke, her companion, was in the circus and spent a great deal of his life in a 1.5 x 1.5 meter box in a home zoo after he growled and became defiant with his trainer due to his treatment.

Jaguars and More Lions

The next two cats we got to know were the jaguars, Amazon and Brazil, a mother and sister duo. They felt very happy and content, and when we asked about how we could support them, we got a very clear message: don't call us, we'll call you.

They told us they would let us know if our assistance was ever needed! As our relationship has deepened, we have come to know them as incredibly powerful, confident beings, and we have partnered with them to support the Amazon and other jaguars.

We were asked to speak with Taai and Beau. It was Taai's birthday. Taai was very animated in his reply:

"Hello, beautiful ladies. I am having a wonderful birthday. I am feeling a great deal of gratitude for my life and my presence here at LLA. I live with like-minded people and fur beings. It is delightful to know that I am safe, loved, and cared for. My heart goes out to the other lions on the planet who do not share my circumstances."

Luke, Carl, and Phuku

One day when we were asked to check on Carl, Luke asked for support. As we were preparing to speak to Carl, Luke came forward. He wanted to share his story with us. He talked about the way he was so cruelly treated by his former people. There was a tremendous amount of sorrow about it. He let us know what a relief it was to tell someone.

He asked for healing, and we combined the conversation with energy work to release trauma from both his body and mind. We did some healing work for Carl next. We both felt like there was some substantial pain in his right hip.

Soon afterward, we were asked to check in on Luke, as well as his partner, Phuku. We shared with Andi that we had a beautiful session. We reported that they were very well matched; they have a lot of affection for each other and are happy to be together.

They both feel very grateful to be at LLA. They feel safe and thankful, and they know not all lions are so fortunate. They both still carry some deep sadness from their pasts. We did some healing work around that with them this morning and will continue to do so at their request.

We spoke with Reign, Sienna, and Shannon as well. Like many of the other cats here, they want to bring healing to animals of all kinds and help shift the relationship between animals and humans on the planet.

Cecil Decides He Enjoys Our Company!

In the meanwhile, our relationship with Cecil continued to progress beautifully. He became quite interested in our lives and how we spent our time outside of LLA.

One day, I was driving to meet Cathy at a sanctuary in Northern California, and I noticed Cecil energetically on the roof of my car! Animals can travel interdimensionally, and he had decided that he wanted to accompany us for a closer look into our lives.

We felt him around us all day at the sanctuary, and in particular when we went out to dinner that evening. We were with another friend, had coconut margaritas, and were having a perfectly hilarious time at one of our favorite restaurants.

When we checked in with Cecil the following week, we received this message:

"Dear ladies, I have been following your antics with great amusement. You have interesting and fun times. I wish you would party and relax more. You take life too seriously. Is there any way I can assist you? You are dear to me, and I wish your lives to be full and happy. My health and my strength are continuing to improve. I am finding great joy and satisfaction."

More Ukranian Cats

Not long afterward, Andi asked us to check in with a number of cats rescued from Ukraine by another organization. She wanted to be sure the cats were in good hands, as there was some concern about their well-being.

With Andi's permission, we asked the LLA cats if any would be interested in supporting the recently rescued cats. This was the beginning of our regularly engaging with the cats to gain support for others in need of help. They did so magnificently. Kanosha, the Tigress, had been connecting to one of the Lionesses. She informed us, "It is very satisfying to be in this role. I have found I have a gift for this and am so delighted with you for opening this connection and avocation for me. This is part of my purpose. I am discovering my powers and magic within myself that I never realized I possessed. It is magnificent. My heart is full. Thank you for helping me come out of my protected shell, so to speak."

Cecil was also in direct contact with the cats and reported that they were adjusting, but that it would take some time. He informed us that the LLA cats were very glad to be able to help and connect with these cats. He reported that it was the beginning of a larger purpose for the cats in the world. "We are building a network of safety and unifying animals across the planet. This is magnificent work and it is so wonderful to be in partnership with you. You have no idea what you mean to us."

Cathy and I were also involved in communicating and sharing healing energy. One of the rescued cats came in to let us know it was a relief to discover that not all humans are bad. She reported that all the cats were benefiting from the healing work and would like more.

While we were working with the cats, a number of giraffes on the property asked to be included. They later came in to thank us. "We are grateful for this beautiful energy you have bestowed upon us. Many blessings to you and your friend."

Collaborating on Planetary Healing Work

The next time we met with the LLA cats, they did not want anything for themselves, but wanted to participate with Cathy and me in some of our broader planetary work for all animals. Our focus that day was healing for all animals in captivity, but we included all animals negatively impacted by humans in any way. It was incredibly beautiful and powerful, and we were grateful to them for suggesting it. It was especially poignant because it was 2/22/22! It was extraordinary to witness not only their own healing and progress, but also their taking their power back by supporting others in similar situations.

Another Ukrainian Rescue

Afterward, Andi connected us with more humans providing sanctuary for cats rescued from Ukraine. It's important to note that even before the Israel-Hamas war took place, Ukraine was a dismal place for zoo animals. Their enclosures were tiny cement blocks for the most part, and care of the animals was suboptimal.

There were a number of ongoing rescue efforts focused on Ukrainian cats. Several cats were being relocated to Spain, and Andi asked if we could support them. Cathy and I spoke with the cats to inform them of the upcoming rescue, addressed their questions and concerns, and asked Andi to share those with the humans involved. They were both relieved and extremely nervous. We shared with Andi that they were doing pretty well considering the circumstances. There was a little survivor's guilt, and we let them know that many folks were working to free them. The conversation definitely helped them, and they seemed to be feeling better.

After they arrived, they informed us that they could feel that the people with them now were kind. They greatly appreciated this. We recognized that they were deeply bonded. When we asked them what kind of healing they wished for themselves, they wanted healing for everyone in Ukraine. Cathy and I had already planned on conducting a similar healing. Cecil joined us and used his roar to send peace and healing through sound. If you're not already aware, sound is the oldest form of healing on the planet and one of the most efficacious.

He Who Writes the Story

In April of 2022, we were asked to reach out to a white lion who would soon be making LLA his home. Umbhali came to Love Lions Alive sanctuary after a veterinarian called them about an unwell cub from a breeding farm. The cub had collapsed due to pain and could not even raise his head. The breeding farm signed him over to the veterinarian to shoot, but the veterinarian instead contacted LLA. They collected the cub and took him to a specialist veterinarian for three weeks of treatment.

His difficulties were a direct result of inbreeding. There are multiple lion farms in South Africa, and most cats end up living in dire circumstances. They go on to make their "owners" money by performing, being petted, or worst of all being sold to a canned hunting facility. Many American so-called "big game hunters" frequent these facilities where they can easily slaughter an animal at close range. Umbhali was fortunate to escape that fate.

Umbhali's good fortune was tempered by the results of the inbreeding. He had a myriad of physical challenges and found it very difficult to move his body, among other unpleasant effects of the human greed that had created him. The other cats were very excited about his arrival and shared with us their intent to support his healing.

Umbhali's name means "he who writes the story." He shared with us, "I really like my new name. It feels majestic and is something I can grow into. I am excited about the life ahead of me. I never thought I would be so privileged. My life has been one of darkness and pain. I am being led into the light. I wish all my brethren could have this experience."

We told him all the cats were looking forward to his arrival, that they believe he is very special, and that they are excited. They are doing some sort of ritual to bring him in. They believe he is the one they have been waiting generations for. Somehow, "he will lead the animals out of the dark and into the light. Lions will regain their rightful place in the world."

Umbhali really appreciated the kindness of the vet and staff and was opening up to the idea that there were worthwhile human beings on the planet. Cecil was especially helpful and supportive in his transition. Cathy and I had been sharing Reiki with Umbhali, but began to engage in deeper healing work with him.

There was a method I had learned in a medical intuitive class that I was anxious to try with him. I had no idea if it would work, but if it did, it could change his life substantially. The day after I conducted the process, Umbhali let Cathy know that all of a sudden, he was able to move much more easily. I was flabbergasted and incredibly excited! It was excruciating to watch this beautiful, sacred being struggle to move.

Nahara and Umbahli's Progress

Soon after Umbahli's arrival, Andi asked us to reach out to a young female cub. She had been orphaned and burned in a fire. She had been confiscated by the National Society for the Prevention of Cruelty to Animals and was slated to go to LLA when she was well enough to travel. We reached out and reassured her that she would be with people she could trust from now on and that she was going to a safe place. She was terrified of returning to where she came from and was quite relieved. Cecil had also been reaching out to her to comfort her and prepare her for her arrival. We shared some Reiki with her, and she was beginning to relax and find some peace.

Soon afterward, we checked in with Umbahli again. He let us know he was doing extremely well. He said, "You can tell Andi that I am doing marvelously! I am becoming accustomed to my new space and enjoying it. I love the way of life here. My body feels free and easy compared to the past, and this brings me much joy. Thanks to all of you for my transformation! I can finally be a real lion!" His energy was very playful and enthusiastic.

A week later, Umbahli reported that he was enjoying his life immensely. He told us he had never imagined being able to play and experience so much joy in life. He is loving it!

Request from the Jaguars

That same week, our beloved LLA jaguar friends, Amazon and Brazil, asked us to send healing to all the jaguars on the planet and to the Amazon. All the LLA cats wanted to participate, and it was incredibly powerful. We could feel the positive impact not only on the jaguars of the Amazon but also on the land itself. We felt the gratitude and the healing taking place. We saw beautiful lights of multiple colors moving into the plants, the Earth, and other living beings.

We were thrilled that the cats wanted to be included in the planetary healing work we had begun the year before. We focused on different species and different challenges each time and were told by the animals involved that it made a tremendous difference.

Umbahli and Nahara Meet

The sweet little lioness arrived at LLA several months later. They named her "Nahara," and she absolutely loved it. We had a very sweet conversation with her. We told Andi, "She is very excited about getting a new name, as you had planned, and she wants something regal to reflect who she is. She is doing well but is anxious to be released from her management (temporary) area. She is a little lonely there. She is excited to have come to you. Cecil, of course, has been reaching out to her, which she greatly appreciates. He is such a wonderful ambassador!"

She was placed next to Umbahli but needed to grow bigger to be placed with him safely. Umbahli was lonely and very impatient to be with her. They were very loving together through the fence line. We explained the situation to Umbahli and reported back to Andi, "He is thrilled to know that he will have multiple opportunities to connect with her close by. One of the things he is really missing and craving is physical touch with another being. Cathy taught him how to connect with Nahara heart-to-heart, and he loved it. We did a heart healing for both of them, which they really enjoyed. We also worked on releasing some trauma for Nahara and enhancing her capacity to feel safe and at peace. We enjoyed them both!"

Connecting with Isindile

In October of 2022, Andi asked if we would be willing to support two cats at a newly opened sanctuary called "Isindile." The first two cats were tigers. This was the beginning of our collaboration. The sanctuary has grown tremendously, and we have made many new and amazing friends. More information is to be found in the following chapter.

Phoenix and the Mountain Lions

Cathy and I live in Central/Northern California and have long been big fans of mountain lions, who are native to our respective counties. We have mountain lion friends at a number of different zoos and sanctuaries. Phoenix is the solo mountain lion at LLA. He lived with his mother, Cleo, originally, but had been alone once she crossed. We had reached out to him, and he began to connect with us more frequently. Cleo began to connect with us as well. She reported that she still watched over the sanctuary and that her energy was very present at LLA.

One day we checked in with the cats, and there was not a lot of feedback or requests for support. We had recently connected with a mountain lion in Los Angeles who had been captured and was believed to be gravely ill. The cats had been very open to connecting with and supporting others of their kind and had made a tremendous difference in the lives of those cats. We asked Phoenix if he was interested in supporting this cat, and they connected.

That day, we ran a healing for all mountain lions, and both Phoenix and Cleo participated. The healing was incredibly powerful and beautiful, and we had a strong sense of how sacred the work was.

We shared the following with Andi: "Phoenix is amazing! He's been connecting with us more and more. Cleo came in too, to help with healing and protection for all the cougars. It was very cool." Andi replied, "Phoenix is amazing. Every time you see Phoenix, you feel a gush of awe and excitement. He engenders respect. Phoenix is amazing." Cathy replied, "We are very honored that he is connecting and communicating with us more frequently and deeply. He is very special. Here where we live, there are a lot of mountain lions. They told us today that because they live in such proximity to humans, they are sort of a bridge to help humans feel more connected to all the big cats, and they hope that will lead to more respect and caring for all the big cats everywhere. It was deep! We asked about mountain lions being solitary animals, and they told us that they are, but they are still all connected through the larger 'puma consciousness' kind of like whales and dolphins. He and Cleo are still very connected too. She watches over him and all of you and is a protector and healer for all the cougars."

Phuku and Nahara Step Up

Nahara and Umbahli had been placed together, and in her excitement to be with another cat and to play, Nahara was becoming far too rough with Umbahli. Even though he had improved remarkably, he was still somewhat physically compromised. We asked the cats for someone to teach Nahara to play gently with him. To our surprise and delight, Phuku stepped in.

Several months later, Cathy and I were supporting two orphaned mountain lion cubs from a nearby local zoo. Phuku had been enjoying her motherly duties with Nahara, so we invited her to help if she wanted. She was not only up for it but excited about it. Nahara jumped in and wanted to help as well.

Both lionesses continued to step up to support others and became deeply connected to their own power and purpose. After everything Phuku has been through, she has become one of the most magnanimous cats we have worked with.

Healing from the Cats

We had developed a deep and loving relationship with all of the LLA cats. We became a family. We met with them every other week and sometimes more frequently. We checked in with Andi prior to each meeting to see if she had questions or concerns about specific cats, and we also asked if any of the other cats had questions or wanted to connect.

We did deeper one-on-one healings as needed and offered an overall healing for the cats at each session. In May of 2023, the cats would not let us do healing work. Instead, they insisted on doing healing work for us. They communicated that they also wanted to support our mission of healing the animals of the planet. The healing was powerful, beautiful, and profound.

Lions Impacted by the Israel/Hamas War

Several months later, Andi asked if we could connect with the lions in Israel and Gaza. There were a great many lions, including quite a few in private residences. Many of them wanted to speak up.

We told Andi, "They are so full of wisdom and courage. They know it's bad there. They know they are not safe. However, they are not afraid. They believe they are there at this time for a purpose. They are meant to be there. They are holding space and grounding energy. They are at peace with this. They are rather fed up in general with humans and what a mess we have made and are making of everything. They also know there are people like us who are trying to make a difference, and that gives them hope."

They wanted to thank Andi for the vision she held for lions and big cats in general for them to be free and to live as they are meant to. They informed us that her vision is felt around the globe and makes a big difference.

Amazon and Brazil Become Healing Ambassadors

Cathy and I had been working with a tiger in a California facility who had been rescued from some pretty dire circumstances. We had been connecting to do healing and to bring comfort and love into her new life. As we always do, once we were certain, we let her know she was in a safe place with people she could trust, which brought her peace.

Some of the harm that had been done to her was irreparable, and she had a leg that was due to be amputated. The morning the amputation was scheduled, Amazon came in and joined us. Amazon herself has three legs and had managed to thrive. She came in to comfort Imara and educate her about what to expect, how to use her body as efficiently as possible, and to give her hope.

Imara was so happy about their connection and friendship, and Amazon was excited to have a friend who shared something so important with her. It was really beautiful to witness them connecting.

Sienna's Challenge

Sienna, a lioness, had not been feeling well, and Cathy and I had been doing some healing work with her, much of it focused on realigning her body, which had somehow become energetically disconnected. Andi reported that she was doing better and that Sienna had even approached her. This was significant because Sienna had avoided Andi somewhat when she wasn't feeling well.

I saw a disturbing image over and over again and realized that Sienna was sending the image to me. We had reported to Andi that something was triggering her past trauma. I explained that she kept showing me herself as a cub with a male lion. We were realigning her body physically, but her lumbar vertebrae, hips, and a couple of cervical vertebrae and hip muscles still kept going out of alignment. There was something more to the story.

One of the main things that kept coming up to clear was fear. It was so intense that it was affecting her digestive system and negatively impacting her desire to eat, which concerned Andi greatly.

Andi asked if I was seeing a really tiny cub just born, or older. It was hard for me to determine, but she was very small in the image. Andi said she was tiny, eyes shut, about the size of my shoe. I received another image of the male looking very intense and appearing aggressive. We continued working on Sienna's body, but again everything we reset kept falling back out of alignment.

Andi informed me that there was a male who had attacked her mother, but he was not in the picture by the time she was born. Several days later, she asked us to check in with Sienna's lioness sibling, Reign. Reign was not doing well. We connected with Reign and reported back that Reign was okay except for her concern about Sienna. Shannon, her brother, was also very concerned.

It seemed that their relationship had changed temporarily, with Sienna isolating herself somewhat. Sienna said to have patience, that she was going through a process. Cathy and I both picked up that she had been suppressing something from the past that was now coming up to be cleared.

We continued to focus on clearing old trauma for Sienna. We checked in a week later, and Sienna said to tell Andi that she was finally turning a corner. She said she had been through a long emotional ordeal that took a toll on her body. She also said that the wounds of her past were now healed.

Reign is much happier and able to resume her normal life. She had been very concerned because Sienna had been down for so long, but she now believes Sienna will be completely healed.

We also worked with Sasha, one of Sienna's siblings. He later told Cathy and me, "You don't realize how big your hearts are and how much your love matters. We have all benefitted greatly. We are very blessed that you have come into our lives."

Rufina

Our beloved Phuku was in the market for more animals to support. We let her know about two lions in Ukraine and asked Andi for suggestions. Andi had recently adopted a young caracal kitten. She informed us that the kitten, Rufina, was orphaned and most likely stolen from her mother after the mother was killed. Caracal mothers are ferociously protective of their young.

We reported back that Rufina was a total sweetheart and very confused about what was happening. She asked about her mother. We explained the situation, but she had a hard time wrapping her head around it. We offered her energy work, and she enjoyed it.

A week later, we connected with Rufina again. Rufina was obviously still really missing her mother. Animals can connect with each other easily, even when they are on the other side. We thought we had connected the two before, but we needed to do more to show Rufina how to connect with her mother's energy. We filled every cell of Rufina's body with her mother's love, then ran more energy to help her feel the connection. She relaxed, and we saw the two of them sitting together.

She said to us excitedly, "You have given me my mother back!" She was very happy. We have worked with a number of recently orphaned animals and have discovered that reconnecting them with their mothers can be very helpful to support their recovery and allow them to begin to thrive.

Deepening Relationships

Umbahli popped in that day to tell us how much he loved us. He felt his strength and power growing and was very excited about it. Nahara came in to say she loves us too. This was very sweet to hear. We receive positive feedback from the cats routinely, and it means so much to us. They mean so much to us. Andi means so much to us. She is a genuine hero, and we feel so blessed to help her in our way.

The White Spirit Lions Make Their Presence Known

In May of 2024, Andi ended her business relationship with a woman who had been helping to care for the cats for a number of years. It was a very difficult and challenging time. We rallied to support her and remind her exactly how much she meant to the LLA cats much more so than the individual who was no longer a part of LLA.

The cats wanted us to let her know that they had her back. They shared beautiful messages with us, and the depth of their love and admiration for Andi was incredible. We saw the cats energetically circled around Andi, sending her love. We told her that they wanted her to know how very much they loved and cared for her and that they were sending her love from their hearts to hers.

We saw beautiful pink light coming from their hearts and penetrating every cell in her body. We let her know we had never heard lions singing before, but they were singing a love song to her in a language we didn't understand. They wanted to heal Andi with their love.

We felt the presence of white spirit lions. They shared the following message with Andi:

"You are one of us. You come from the stars and shine so brightly. Never allow another to dim your light. We have seen what you have accomplished, and it is magnificent. The difference you make is felt all over the world by every lion being. There is true greatness within you. We believe in you. Know that you have our blessing and support. Know that you have accomplished great things!"

The next week, when we checked in with the cats, Nahara had a lot to say in reference to our Monday session. She said, "Yesterday was very exciting for all of us. I got to help Andi heal, and that was amazing!" She was also excited that Andi saw how special and powerful she is. She wants to do more and believes that the sky is the limit. She understands that this is the beginning of something very big.

She is excited to be a part of the healing and said that one of the reasons she came to you was that Umbahli is a part of the big stuff too. She said the two of them were meant to be together to do major healing work on the planet. Their missions are intertwined. She let us know that Umbahli has deep wisdom and healing to offer, but he is more quiet and reserved. She emphasized that it is important to listen to him because he is so wise.

We shared that Azi was excited about the work we did together and wants to do more. Cecil said he is very pleased and that his heart is very full. We let her know that he was going to be a big part of hers and the planetary healing Cathy and I have been engaging in. He says this is a big turning point for all the cats. And it's important to him that you know he is loving you, supporting you, and has your back for everything you are doing. He has tremendous gratitude toward you. We were also told that more and more cats would be joining in the work.

Cathy and I are both certified Dolphin–Whale healers and have brought them in a number of times to support the cats. When we were doing healing work with the cats, one day soon afterward, we asked that the energy be shared with Andi as well. It was beautiful, and we saw some really amazing things that we shared with her:

"All of your chakras were clearing and your energy field was spinning. Your Merkaba, your light body, was being activated. It's your vehicle to take you from the physical world into the spiritual. It is said to align you with your supreme being and supports you to align fully with your purpose and passion!"

The Fire

In the summer of 2024, there was a fire at LLA. It destroyed some of the enclosures and the greenery within them. Both Odin and Cecil were burned, and our sweet little serval kitten, Rufina, perished in the fire. She had been doing remarkably well, moving past her grief, and the day we reconnected her with her mother's energy was extremely moving and beautiful. We comforted ourselves with the knowledge that she was now reunited with her mother for eternity. Andi's home was destroyed, and she moved into the little cottage she had been using as an office.

The Surgery

Later that month, Nahara was to be spayed. All the female LLA cats were spayed to prevent more lions from being born into captivity. Nahara was quite upset and disappointed. She very much wanted to have babies and would have been an extraordinary mother.

My kittens had surgery several months later. My little Angel came through it with flying colors. My sweetie, Prince, had a harder time not physically, but emotionally. I didn't realize it at the time, but later another healer pointed out to me that he was very upset that I hadn't asked for his input prior to making the decision. I had informed him about the upcoming surgery and its purpose, but I didn't realize how he felt about it. He may have tried to communicate with me about it, but I may have failed to hear his words.

I explained to him that there were more cats in the U.S. than there were homes, but it took him a bit of time to recover. I will never take spaying or neutering a cat so lightly again.

Sasha's Passing

Not too long afterward, beautiful Sasha, a white male lion, lost his fight with cancer. Cathy ran a healing for everyone. First, she saw many pink dolphins come in. They were healing Andi's heart and the hearts of all the cats. Then she saw a pink dolphin guide come in to guide Sasha home.

"I saw them going through the stars, the galaxies, the planets side by side. I saw changing colors, a lot of stars, celestial stuff like glitter. Then Sasha and the dolphin both turned golden. Then a very large white lion I was told he was the 'oversoul' of the lions came in to guide Sasha the rest of the way home into the starry galaxy where he is from. I saw the same when I connected with him."

Cathy went on to say, "I had a very clear feeling of time having no meaning. Hard to explain: everything happens instantly and also constantly. There is no time and space, there just IS."

Sasha had a message for Andi: "I know my beloved humans are sad, and really there is no reason to be sad. I have not died! I just changed form. I've done it many times before we all have and I will do it many times again." He was sort of sad to leave this physical body because it was so "gorgeous magnificent." He was really proud of that body he had created. But then he said, "It's OK. I will just create an even more magnificent body next time. Wait till you see it!"

We let Andi know that he would be a lion again and most likely a white lion. "He will always be with you and may come back to you as another lion." I told Andi that I saw Sasha snuggling with her and rubbing against her. So much love. He said he would send her messages in the form of white feathers. I saw the White Lions come to get him, and the most beautiful gold light was coursing through his body. Cathy added, "I love that we both saw the White Lions and his golden body."

The Magic of the Jaguars

Andi had been approached by an acquaintance about holding an spiritual ceremony journey on the mountain because it was such a sacred place energetically. Around this time, we were becoming more aware of how incredibly powerful the two LLA jaguars, Amazon and Brazil, truly were. They described themselves as very sacred and powerful spiritual beings. They were shamans and healers in other lifetimes. They had been, thus far, unable to fulfill that part of their purpose in this lifetime.

The mountain is also very sacred, powerful, and spiritual, as is the energy there. The jaguars were excited about this ceremony and felt that being there with us and participating in that kind of work helped them fulfill their soul purpose.

Around the same time, Andi wrote a Facebook post about Nahara and her journey. Nahara was very aware of it and totally in her element with her newfound fame. We shared with Andi that Nahara knew about the splash she had made on social media. She said, "Finally, my story has been told. I am a star. I am famous, and everyone knows how special I am!" She was absolutely beside herself.

We asked Andi how the ceremony went. It was a tremendous success. Everyone enjoyed it, and Andi experienced some deep and interesting insights about herself and her life.

We shared with Andi that Amazon and Brazil understood that they were critical to the success of the ceremony. "They helped you have all of your revelations. They helped you get more fully into your power. They shared that your transformation is beneficial not only to the LLA cats, but to all cats. They have been reunited with their roots, culture, and power as well. The ceremony helped them more fully step into their power and fulfill their purpose more deeply.

"They really liked the guy who led the event. They felt he was respectful of their wisdom and recognized their power. They are looking forward to creating more good for you and LLA. They see this as a turning point."

Summer

In December 2024, Andi was contacted about a little lioness who was being passed around in an Egyptian market. She had been taken from her mother to bring in some cash for the man who decided to ruin her life to make a buck. He charged people to hold her, pet her, and spend time with her. Two women who ran an equine sanctuary purchased her to save her from a very unpleasant fate.

When we first connected with Summer, we reported the following to Andi:

"When we checked in with Summer, she felt a little timid, but we did not pick up any fear. She understands that she is now safe and that she will have a home where she can be with other lions and hear them roar. She is currently being treated very kindly. She was always afraid before and was treated roughly. She was taken from her mother and her heart is yearning for her. Nahara came in to support her. She was very relieved. We could see Nahara licking her and rubbing her head with hers. She will mother her and teach her how to be a lioness."

Summer was thrilled to be out of her buyer's clutches, as well as away from the pawing market attendees. However, she did not feel understood as a lion and was anxious to be with her own kind and others who would understand her. It took quite some time before the permits for her travel were issued. She was on her way to get on a plane to LLA when there was an issue with the paperwork. She was held and placed into a petting zoo of all places before being sent back to the equine sanctuary, and the process began again.

When Summer finally arrived at LLA, she settled in quickly. She bonded with Andi immediately, as if they were always meant to be together. It is our deep belief that they have been together in many other lifetimes. She was surrounded by lions and in touch with who she was for the very first time since she had been ripped away from her mother. The lions were roaring even more frequently than they had done before.

We checked in with Summer soon after her arrival and reported to Andi:

"Summer is super happy! She let us know her life is even better than what we described to her. The other lions have been very accepting and welcoming to her, like big brothers and sisters. She thinks you are an angel. This is the person she was meant to be with. We feel so much love when she speaks about you. She understands that you love her, just wasn't clear why she can't be with you all the time. Cathy did a great job of explaining. We told her she can connect with your heart anytime she wants to. This is the first time she has ever experienced so much love. She finally feels like she is in a place where lions belong and the people there understand lions. Cathy showed her how to connect heart to heart and we felt her doing it. I got a sense of how much she looks up to Nahara. We let her know that she would have a friend someday."

Essie's Struggles

Andi had told us about a tiny lioness she had named Essie, living in a country in Northern Africa. A woman at a local camp was caring for her. It would be some time before Essie could come to LLA permits were difficult to obtain, and many other arrangements were needed to make the journey possible.

In early May, Essie's caretaker, contacted Andi to let her know that Essie was missing. She had been in a meeting and, when she returned, Essie was nowhere to be found. She had placed her in a part of the camp she enjoyed spending time in and had left her there for only one hour. They could not find any holes in the fence from which she might have escaped. The camp was in the bush, and there were many hyenas roaming at night. Sweet Essie was in danger. Cathy and I both tried to connect and could not feel her energy at all. We began to run energy to help her find her way back to the camp.

In the meantime, sweet Luke had been suffering from some digestive challenges. When I did some energy work for him, I picked up that he had been exposed to some sort of toxin. Andi later discovered that, unbeknownst to LLA, one of the carcasses that Luke had eaten had been injected with something just prior to the animal's death. Luke says he is quite well and has improved remarkably. I ran some energy to address the toxin and Cathy and I both did several sessions for him.

When we checked in several days later, he told us,

"Hats off to you ladies for this work. You are magnificent and have improved my outlook on life!"

Cathy had picked up that Essie was scared and might be hiding. The following day, Andi informed us that a young boy had found Essie far from camp.

"A group tried to catch her, but she was running away from them, so they circled her until She came and brought her back home. She was extremely weak and could not stand up. She tried to move, but her body didn't respond. She did drink water and ate a tiny bit of fresh meat."

Cathy and I began to support her with healing work and to release the trauma she had suffered.

The next day, we were informed that Essie had disappeared again. We had previously asked if there were any animals in camp that might be able to shed some light on what had happened, but Essie had returned home before we had the opportunity.

Essie's caretaker informed Andi that there was a reedbuck hanging around the camp trying to get her attention after Essie's second disappearance. This same being had been near Essie's enclosure. Cathy and I reached out. This beautiful being was very distraught and showed both of us two humans who had been in close proximity to Essie. Someone had taken her from her enclosure.

Cathy and I began doing energy work almost immediately for her protection, safe return, and healing. We worked on this separately since we were not able to meet that day.

It was clear that there were humans in the village who did not want Essie around, as small and relatively harmless as she was at the time. Fortunately, she was found again. She placed a guard at her enclosure. She explained to the villagers again that this was a temporary situation and that Essie would be coming to LLA as soon as the paperwork was in place.

Cathy had witnessed a beautiful healing for Essie and shared the following:

"I was on a call this morning where we do a group meditation with whales and dolphins. They took me to an underwater temple that was like Lemurian. Essie was there, and they put her on a throne and did a big healing. I was told that she was a priestess back in Lemurian days and, for some reason, was cast out. So all of this being 'cast out' I think is clearing past life karma and agreements. That had to be done before she can come to LLA.

"Toward the end, they put a crown on her and said she is a High Priestess in this lifetime. Fascinating, combined with what you did, Cindie. Hoping now that we cleared all this up, maybe the path will open for her to come to LLA. Also did the pink bubble thing, and there were many whales, dolphins, and white lions. It was like a ceremony and also protection. It was beautiful, and they said this is the world we are creating, and we are all part of it the three of us, Essie, and all at LLA."

Cecil's Progress

Cecil, who is now called Rasta, had lived alone since coming to LLA. He had a tremendous amount of physical healing to do before he was ready to share his space.

We checked in with him and informed Andi that Rasta would definitely like some companions. He explained that he was going through a deep healing process. He liked the idea of being with the three ladies, but wanted to make sure they were okay with it.

When we checked in with the lionesses who had been chosen for Rasta, they were very open to the idea and shared that they have a tremendous amount of respect for him. They said he is very kind, gentle, and respectful with them. He has a big heart and is a very special lion. They realize it will be an adjustment, but they are well-settled and ready. They have admired Rasta for a long time and would be honored to share space with him.

Summer's Transformation

Summer had expressed interest in more healing work. What came through in her session surprised and delighted me! I asked for guidance and heard, "Run the energy of belonging and activate her full lioness powers!"

It was super cool! She was surrounded by six white spirit lions. I saw energy from them going into her brain and then her heart. It is her greatest desire to be a "real" lioness, and with this, there can be no more doubt that is exactly who she is.

After Summer's healing, three white spirit lions appeared to me and let me know that it was time for them to help me with my beloved horse family.

There are three horses (formerly four) that I have traveled from lifetime to lifetime with. I have known some of them for close to ten years. They belong to a friend who formerly lived near me but has moved four hours away. We have a connection that is incredibly powerful, and I travel to see them once a month. It is my dearest wish to spend the rest of my lives with them in close proximity. I think and pray about this on a daily basis. They mean everything to me.

Prophecies

Almost exactly ten years ago, a psychic friend of mine talked about the work I was doing with animals and said that when three of us connected and made a commitment to supporting animals together, the world would change and become a better place for all non-human beings.

For many years, we believed the third was our friend Claudia. We spent a lot of time together sharing healing and communication at sanctuaries and zoos. We had planned to come together to formally make the commitment, but Claudia moved out of the area soon afterward, and it never took place.

For a number of years, we shared similar experiences with a third mutual friend, but it turned out that she was not the one either.

Cathy had a vision that confirmed things   Andi was our third friend. Tricia's prophecy was coming to pass.

Little did we realize, there was a similar prophecy among the cats about the role we were to play in their future.

Isindile Chapter

In October of 2022, Andi asked us for support for a new big cat sanctuary called Isindile, which was founded and is run by Ansa and David Gerber. As in the beginning with LLA, our first two cats were tigers. Their names were Amber and Or. They had come from a lion park in South Africa. They had arrived several days earlier but were hiding out in the bushes and had not eaten anything. David and Ansa were quite concerned.

We reached out to do some communication and healing work the following day. The cats were very happy to receive it and to be informed that they were in a safe place. They were not used to interacting with kind people, didn't fully understand why they were at the sanctuary, and were worried they would have to go back.

The Isindile tigers Igor and Kanosha as well as Cecil and Nahara, came in to comfort and reassure them. The idea of being safe was new to them. We encouraged them to eat. They explained that they would like their food put out when it was dark and activities had ceased for the day at the sanctuary. They did not want to be watched while eating. We recommended placing the food in a more secluded and sheltered place.

Andi reported to us several days later that the tigers were a lot better and that Amber and Or came out to eat in front of David and Ansa. Or was reported to be shyer. Both walked around their enclosure at night, under cover of darkness. We learned that tigers are typically more shy and secretive around humans.

Andi suggested to Ansa and David that they do a cleansing of the land to remove any negative imprints the tigers might be feeling from hunting on the property, among other things. Cathy and I did a clearing process and checked in the following day. We were informed that the tigers were adjusting well and doing better. They were a little lonely, and we showed them how to connect with the LLA cats. Cecil, Igor, and Kanosha came in again, and that helped tremendously. We did more clearing of the land with respect to hunting and human battles over the area as well. That helped lighten the energy of the sanctuary further.

More Tigers Arrive

We didn't hear again from the Gerbers until eighteen months later. I received the following message from Ansa:

"Through Andi from Love Lions Alive, you made contact with our two tigers, Amber and Or, when we rescued them in 2022. The feedback you gave us was extremely valuable. It helped us understand how they experienced being rescued and how we could be there for them in a way that helped them adjust to their new life.

In the last two weeks, we've rescued three tigers a young male from Pakistan and two white tigers (male and female) from here in

South Africa. Would it be possible for you to reach out to them to do some healing and give us feedback on what they need and how they are feeling? Especially the white male tiger needs healing. I also have a question for all three of them. I need to know how they feel about their current names. Names are extremely important to us."

We checked in with the new cats and reported the following to Ansa and David: They are all very happy to be at Isindile. We look forward to connecting more with them and with you.

Ansa replied, "Wow, I'm feeling really emotional now. It is always so good to hear they are happy to be here. Thank you so much."

Cathy informed her, "It is our pleasure and honor! They are very happy and thankful, and they feel your love. They are very special. We got very emotional too when we connected with them. Amber and the three lions who had been rescued previously joined in as well they are all really happy to be there, and they all have really big hearts. We did a lot of heart healing for the three new tigers. More to come."

I was our notetaker and reported to Ansa:

From your new white male tiger:

"Life was much harder for us than people realize. We are very thankful to be here. Ansa and David are wonderful people. I need time to rest and recover. I appreciate their patience with me and ask for that patience and space to continue. I am ready to leave the past behind completely, to start a brand-new life. I'm very hopeful for a beautiful future filled with love and joy. They took us in and gave us a home when we were at our lowest point."

He expressed that they thought they were going to die before coming. "We feel very happy and safe. We cannot express our gratitude enough!"

From his sister:

"I feel safe. I would like to thank them for rescuing us from a life of hell and torture. We were treated like objects. We were not loved. We were status symbols. The people were horrible, and I feel great anger at the way we were treated. These beautiful people came into our lives and are making us whole the way we were always meant to live.

My gratitude is immense. I have never known humans to be lovable, but these two are an exception. God bless them both for who they are and what they do. They are angels of the highest order."

From Baboo:

"Hello, Divine Sisters. Anyone that wants to help is a friend. I am pleased and delighted with my life in this beautiful place. I feel love all around me and the contentment that we all share here. Life is wonderful. I want for nothing. They are doing everything perfectly. I could not be happier."

We reported back on the tigers' feelings about their names:

"Baboo wants something other than his two names. He trusts you to choose one. The others aren't really clear on what they are being called now, but anything other than the names they came with will be fine. They want no association with the past.

They shared that they never thought they would be able to live at a place like this or find such joy in their lives. Life is beautiful and sacred here. We feel very relieved to feel safe and loved. We have never felt that before.

Amber wanted to relay how happy she is to have other cats here. She said she is doing quite well and doesn't need healing but would like some."

The names chosen for the brother and sister were **Asmir** and **Sahara**, and the male tiger was called **Yehudah**.

We continued to support the group with energy work, and one day did a big heart healing for everyone. When we checked in on Yehudah again, I kept hearing the song *"Happy Days Are Here Again."* He was so enthusiastic. He said:

"My life is wonderful, delightful, amazing, stupendous, fantastic! I never imagined I could have such a life!"

David and Ansa let us know that all the cats were making remarkable progress.

Trouble in Paradise

Not long after Yehudah arrived, he was grating on the nerves of Amber, the first rescue and the "Queen" of Isindile. David and Ansa were aware of her irritated state and asked us to speak with her.

We relayed the following: "Amber let us know that he is bossy and trying to take over and she is right. He has been goading her and telling her he is the favorite. Yehudah admitted it! He explained that he was nervous about being accepted, and we believe it is bravado related to insecurity. Amber shared that everyone thinks he's wonderful, but she sees his true colors. She doesn't have an issue with the other cats because they know their place."

Cathy and I communicated that there was no need for her to like Yehudah just to accept that he is there. We told the Gerbers, "Amber was really relieved. She has been feeling badly about the whole thing. When we told her we would share this with you, she was even more relieved and very happy to hear that. She has been feeling a bit misunderstood."

We did a process to help both keep their energies separate and afterwards did some work on Yehudah's insecurities. Amber became much happier and more at peace, and we were thrilled. She crossed over the Rainbow Bridge later in the year. We were devastated to see her go, but relieved and happy she was reunited with her beloved sister Or, who had crossed over before her.

More New Arrivals

A male and female lion cub, Simba and Nala, arrived and we did some energy work with them, but it was not necessary to do much. They were happy to be at Isindile and settled in quickly.

It took a bit longer with the two tigresses that arrived not long afterwards, Leila and Sarabi. They had been owned by an individual who had become aware that captivity was not the best route for them. They were sisters, had suffered from the ill effects of irresponsible breeding, and had some difficulty adjusting at first. We initially believed they were mourning the loss of their person but later discovered they felt differently.

We did some healing work for them and also helped David and Ansa reconnect with Amber and her sister Or. Several days later, we received the following message from David:

"Ansa and I just wanted to thank you both so very much for all your kindness and support with Isindile. Friday's session with you, Amber, Or, Leila, and Sarabi meant so much to us. It was absolutely fantastic listening to Amber communicating to us through you.

It was obviously very emotional (having only buried Amber a few hours before), but brought us great peace and a better understanding of the circle of life. We have no doubt that Amber (and Or) will play a crucial role in guiding us into the future with our plans for the sanctuary.

Remarkably, since our chat, we have seen quite a positive transformation in Leila and Sarabi over the weekend. It's been another tranquil weekend here, with just the two of us, all alone with the big cats. Suddenly, they are exploring much more of their enclosure and are settling into a routine with their eating.

We put up two camera traps (one on either side of the enclosure), and the footage shows them moving around all night long! Although there is still the usual growling, it seems less aggressive and more out of habit. They definitely seem a bit calmer in our presence. We'll keep you updated on their progress."

Soon afterwards, Leila and Sarabi informed us that they held deep wisdom and that it was part of their life purpose to be at Isindile.

At a later check-in with Leila and Sarabi, they informed us of the following:

"We are beginning to warm up to these beautiful people and this place. We are feeling safe and relieved. We are beginning to experience the joy of being a tiger in the natural world."

They shared more about their former person:

"He used us. He was not abusive, but we were just objects to him. We thought that's what humans were like. We did not want more of it. We are learning that humans can be good and are more open to connecting. It will still take time, but progress is being made.

These people are so different. It is a delight and a relief that they are not like him."

Sadly, not long afterwards, Sarabi died from the health-related impacts of irresponsible breeding practices. Leila was devastated but soon began to thrive without the burden of her constant worry about Sarabi's well-being.

A Change of Plans for the Isindile Pride

During this time period, the Gerbers planned to bring three more cats under their loving care from a facility in Spain. There was a leopard called Brave and a lion and lioness called Sem and Liena.

In the meantime, some challenges surfaced in the Isindile pride, which was currently composed of a lioness and two lions. David explained that the brothers had started fighting with Bina, the female. They were reaching sexual maturity and also sensed Bina's weakness because she only had three legs and had difficulty defending herself.

A decision was made to place her siblings in a separate but adjacent enclosure so they could maintain their relationships safely. Their relationship thrived under the new arrangement.

The White Spirit Lions Bring Healing

We were asked to help explain the decision to the pride to support them in their new configuration. We reported to David and Ansa the following:

"We had an amazing session with the Isindile pride this morning. We were trying to explain what happened with them and decided to call in our White Spirit Lions for support. It feels like they have a much better understanding and are at peace with it.

We ran a healing for the three of them as individuals and their relationship. It was really beautiful! We saw all kinds of beings come in to support them. We saw their hearts being healed, their bonds being repaired, and an incredibly beautiful flow of love between them."

David was curious about the White Spirit Lions, and Cathy shared that white lions are very powerful spiritual beings and healers both those on the planet and those in spirit.

"You can think of the White Spirit Lions sort of like we would think of spirit guides. They are very powerful healers and guides and also help us heal the planet. Linda Tucker has written a couple of good books if you are interested."

I added that while it's been some time since I read Linda Tucker's amazing book (which Cathy turned me onto), titled *Mystery of the White Lions*, I highly recommend it. I explained that they are said to be a bridge between the physical and spiritual worlds. In some myths, white lions in general are said to have supernatural powers and come from the Sun God. They are also said to be stewards of physical transformation during times of transition.

They appear to Cathy and me when we are working with animals, primarily the big cats, and some others support us in our healing work. They don't appear to everyone, but they have let us know how much they appreciate and respect the work we are doing. They support and help us and the animals we are working with. They are in another dimension.

They also come in when we work with Andi. They believe her to be one of a select few who truly understand lions what they need and how they should be managed. They first came to us when we were working with the LLA cats and now appear outside of that, sometimes even with domestic animals. The work they do with us is astounding. We are really good at what we do, but when they come in, what happens is beyond even our capabilities. We were struggling to explain the dynamics to the Isindile pride and asked them to help.

David chimed in that white lions are also very powerful spirits in African culture. An interesting fact that you might know: unlike the hundreds (if not thousands) bred in captivity for man's exploitation, there are currently only four wild white lions walking this planet three of them in the Timbavati and one (Casper) in the Satara area.

A Leopard Named Brave

Our work with leopards until this time had been relatively limited. Love Lions Alive (LLA) had rescued a leopardess named Cali. She had been captured by humans and kept in horrific conditions in a small, filthy trailer before she was eventually rescued. Andi placed her at LLA's Limpopo facility, where she was fed and cared for in a large wild area so that she wouldn't become accustomed to humans and could eventually be returned to the wild.

We loved her and checked in with her from time to time. She was grateful to have been removed from her situation and was enjoying her newfound freedom. Andi took care to ensure she had the most minimal contact possible with humans. She was fed regularly, with the hope that she would resume hunting eventually.

Cali was at the facility for some time, and the decision was made that she was ready to be returned to the wild. Permission was granted by the authorities. We checked in after her release, and she was beginning to hunt, but requested some support with food for the time being. Not long afterward, she was killed by a poacher.

We grieved for her but comforted ourselves with the fact that she was at least able to live her life with the freedom she so richly deserved, if only for a time. She had a beautiful disposition, and we enjoyed connecting with her and supporting her with healing energy.

In early February of 2025, David and Ansa informed us that they had a leopard arriving that week. He was another cat kept as a pet in Ukraine and abandoned during the war. When we checked in with Brave, he was still somewhat groggy from his travels. When we explained to him what his new life would be like and that he would never be in chains again, he had a bit of a hard time believing it was true at first. There were tears and so much emotion when he understood.

His message to us was as follows:

"Good morning, lovely ladies. It's so good to meet you. Your support was so beneficial on this very arduous journey. I feel deeply at peace. I don't really know Ansa and David yet, but I can feel their energy and I can feel that their hearts are filled with love.

For all the big cats, and for me in particular, I have been weeping endlessly since you informed me that my life was about to take a major change. God bless whoever has helped me on this journey. My life has been one of hell, of abandonment, of fear, of warfare. But now, I am home. And now, I have the opportunity not to be a pet, but to be simply who I am to touch the grass, to smell the breeze, to see others of my kind, or at least like me, brings me great joy.

I am very exhausted, more than I have ever been; however, my heart is full, my spirit is hopeful, and yes you may publish this.

I know that you will be writing a book about the cats. This gives me great pleasure. I am very excited and wish to be a major participant in this endeavor. It pleases me greatly that you are taking this great life-saving, world-altering work out into the world more broadly. The time has come. This work must be shared. This must be a priority for both of you for the time being.

There is much to be done, and your work will support and save many. The animals of this world have faith in you. They understand that you are pure of heart, that you wish for nothing other than our happiness and well-being, and for justice for all the animals of this planet wild and domestic.

This will be a great collaboration between us. I have much to say and share. You might say that I would like to take the lead in this project, if you will allow me. I am anxious to get some rest now. Please thank these beautiful people for all they have done to bring me home.

I will say it again I am *home*. I have always longed for home, but I have never known what that is, where it was, or what it would look like. I cannot wait to explore, to meet my fellow residents, and to simply be a leopard.

God bless you both for all you do. God bless Ansa and David for all they have done."

His energy was beautiful and magnificent. We understood immediately that he was a very high, powerful being. We came to understand that Brave was to become an important part of both our lives and our work in the world. He was very anxious for us to get moving on the book and was keeping Cathy up at night with his enthusiasm!

Reunited with Our Pride

Sem and Liena arrived at Isindile in March of 2025. Liena was reported to be very bold and Sem very shy, but when they arrived, we found their roles were reversed. Cathy connected with them before I did. She reported the following:

"I just got done connecting with Liena and Sem. A lot of different thoughts and emotions understandably. The trip took a lot out of them. They are tired.

They do understand that this is their forever home they already love it. It's beautiful and peaceful. They are still adjusting, of course, but they know this is a safe place. They know this is a place where they will know peace and safety like they've never known before.

They are very thankful to be here. Sem feels somewhat responsible for Liena and her well-being. He always has, and he took on a lot of responsibility when they were in Ukraine and the other place. They did not feel safe, and he felt the need to protect her.

He can feel they are safe here and that he will be able to relax more than he ever has before. It's very beautiful."

David reported back to us:

"Hope you're both well. In our opinion, your feedback on Sem and Liena is spot on! We were told that Liena is the more dominant one and that Sem is very shy and reserved. But he has definitely settled quicker than Liena, and the roles seem reversed. He is very relaxed, loving our company, and has such an amazing aura about him. He reminds me of Mtazamaji gentle, but with a powerful presence.

Even at feeding time, he is taking his meat first, while we were told that Liena completely dominates and might even try to steal his food. But considering what they've just been through, they both seem very relaxed. Considering it was their first night here, and so far removed from what they have previously known, it was amazing that they roared so loudly and confidently.

What was awesome was that it got Atlarela and Mtazamaji roaring like we have never heard before. Even our neighbor sent a message to say he hears lots of roaring and his house is 3 km away!"

He went on to say:

"In nature, male lions are kicked out of the pride by their father at around two to three years old. They become nomadic and, for the first time in their lives, have to fend for themselves. They move around under the cover of darkness until around five years old, when they are strong and confident enough to take on other male lion coalitions. So normally, they do not move into a new place and start roaring to announce their arrival until they have the confidence to do so.

I know this is not wild nature, but Isindile is as close to being wild as a captive big cat can be. So for them to start roaring on the first day here is nothing short of amazing. It tells him they are old souls with strong instinctual feelings that they are safe, belong here, and that this is their home. And so, they roar to lay claim to their new territory!"

The next time we connected with Sem, the information he shared with us was powerful. It's important to understand what he had to say to better understand our impact on animals and how to support them more effectively. He said:

"I am living a most delightful life, filled with joy and freedom. I am most delighted with my circumstances. The humans here are incredibly kind, patient, and ethical. I trust them completely. This gives me great peace.

I never expected to have a life in which I wasn't treated like a prisoner shut down and being punished for who I am. I was not allowed to be a lion. This caused an identity crisis for me. How could I go on pretending to be someone or something I simply was not?

What humans wanted from me was not reasonable. They wanted me to give up my lion nature and become more like them. I am most pleased. I am finally allowed to be who I am.

If I were to live only one more day, I would die a lion, and I would be at peace. This is the greatest injustice done to animals by humans. They want to take away our very soul and make us fit into their box. Humans can be incredibly inhuman and inhumane. Our species are suffering all over the world.

God bless those who truly see us and give us permission to live our lives the way we were meant to be. God bless David and Ansa. The four of you were the first to recognize me as a lion, and for that I am eternally grateful.

I have been seen, and it means more to me than anyone can possibly realize. My message to humans is this: see us, respect us, give us the freedom we deserve. We are more critical to the human race than you can possibly imagine. Your well-being and our well-being are intricately entwined. When you bless us, you bless yourselves."

Liena settled in and is enjoying her life at Isindile, venturing out more and more every day.

It's important to bring attention to the plight of animals in war zones. Not only are they traumatized and sometimes injured by the consistent bombing, but many of their humans abandon them or set them loose on the streets. In Liena's case, the soldiers actually called a sanctuary to ask if they should shoot her to release her from her plight or if the sanctuary had the capacity to take her in.

A substantial number of people in Israel keep lions as pets. Lions are in private homes all over the world. Until very recently, you could buy a lion cub on the side of the road in a number of U.S. states. Thankfully, that practice has now been outlawed.

Cathy and I had an immediate and intense emotional response to them, as well as to Brave. Sem said to us soon after they arrived:

"We remember the time that we were together. The two of you were always the leaders. You were good leaders just leaders and we all thrived under your leadership. You have our undying, unconditional, and lifelong love and respect."

We had been reunited with our pride.

He also informed us:

"It is time for you to step into your leadership role again."

He revealed that part of their reason for coming to Isindile was to connect with us again. This was what Brave had conveyed to us as well. Brave informed us that Sem, Liena, he, Cathy, and I were going to be a powerful group and step up the work that Cathy and I had begun.

Yehuda and the Babes

This chapter would not be complete without the following story to give you a sense of how diverse animals are within species.

When Yehuda originally arrived, Amber was the only other tiger at Isindile. Since that time, the gorgeous Sahara, Leila, and for a time Sarabi have come into his view.

At a recent check-in with Yehuda, he informed us:

"I am delighted to have such fine ladies in my view. What magnificent babies we would make if circumstances were different. They are total eye candy. When I say this, I mean I see this through the heart, not my eyes. My world is expanding, and I am delighted. I am already blissfully happy here, and it just keeps getting better!"

Threats Big Cats Face and How to Help

The Status of Big Cats

While all big cat species are designated, at a minimum, as vulnerable, more tiger species than any other are considered to be critically endangered. The number of big cats in the wild varies widely depending on who is estimating. The data I am using is from the World Wildlife Fund, one of the most credible sources of wildlife data on the planet.

Big Cat Conservation Status and Numbers in the Wild[1]

Species	Status	Numbers in the Wild
Bengal Tiger[2]	Endangered	5,574
Siberian Tiger	Critically Endangered	400
Sumatran Tiger[3]	Critically Endangered	300
Lion	Vulnerable	20-25,000
Amur Leopard	Critically Endangered	84
Clouded Leopard	Endangered	3700-5580

---

[1] Data was gathered primarily from the World Wildlife Federations datasets

[2] There are six additional species of Tigers, most of which are critically endangered

[3] the data comes from the International Tiger Project. They are there on the ground with the cats and are the best source of information.

Arabian Leopard	Critically Endangered	<200
Snow Leopard	Vulnerable	4,000-6500
Jaguars	Near Threatened	173,000
Cheetahs[4]	Vulnerable	6500

The tigers are particularly concerned there will be no turning back unless more effective, immediate, and consistent action is taken. They have approached Cathy and me with their grave concerns about their future and asked for our support.

Major Threats to Big Cats

The major threats to lions, tigers, and other big cats across the globe are similar. They include:

➤ Habitat loss

➤ Loss of genetic diversity

➤ Decline in the abundance of natural prey

➤ Human–wildlife conflict

➤ Poaching

➤ The illegal wildlife/exotic animal trade

➤ Canned hunting

➤ Breeding and related unethical and harmful practices

➤ Unethical organizations masquerading as sanctuaries

Habitat Loss

---

[4] the data comes from the International Tiger Project. They are there on the ground with the cats and are the best source of information.

For lions specifically, the World Wildlife Federation estimates they inhabit only eight percent of their former range. Tigers, leopards, jaguars, and cheetahs are struggling with the same issue. It is less clear for snow leopards, since vast areas of their habitat have not yet been explored. The irresponsible destruction of the Amazon rainforest is of special concern for jaguars.

Loss of Genetic Diversity

Many big cats live in areas with no protections and are becoming increasingly isolated from one another, which makes it difficult to breed and negatively impacts gene pools. This can lead to inbreeding. The lack of genetic diversity is linked to multiple health problems and other challenges. Additional issues are created by unethical breeders, which is addressed in another section.

Decline in the Abundance of Natural Prey

Food sources are becoming more limited as natural prey declines due to unsustainable development. A recent trend of interest by humans in bushmeat has resulted in a further decline of available food sources.

Breeders and Unethical Practices

It should be noted that all breeders masquerade as organizations helping to repopulate cats in the wild. Nothing could be further from the truth. Their governments will not allow these cats to be released into the wild, and even if that were a possibility, the irresponsible way these cats are bred and the potential detrimental impact on wild populations ensures this will never happen.

While the geographic isolation of big cats from one another negatively impacts genetic diversity, inbreeding is also connected with canned hunting and other forms of using animals for profit. The results can be horrific, and the animals suffer greatly for the duration of their often too-short lives. Our beloved tiger friend Sarabi died as a result of inbreeding and had multiple health problems over the course of her life. Our beloved Umbahli was also a victim of inbreeding and had great difficulty moving normally until he received energy work. He still struggles.

It should also be noted that there is quite a bit of irresponsible breeding going on in the United States. One such example is breeding tigers with lions to create "ligers" and other hybrid animals. These hybrids most often suffer from very poor health and a number of unintended consequences.

These breeders are involved in the bone trade, as well as supplying animals to canned hunting facilities. They literally skin big cats and sell their pelts as rugs. They boil down the cats and harvest their bones to send to countries around the world to be used in traditional forms of medicine.

These breeders are only out to make money from the cats. They lack any sort of conscience and will breed lionesses with known health issues, who may collapse and die during childbirth or pregnancy. Most will not call a vet if an animal is ill and instead let the cats suffer or kill them outright because they are no longer of use.

Human–Wildlife Conflict / Retaliatory Killing

As humans begin to inhabit former big cat territories, they are competing with cats for space and resources. When big cats enter human-occupied areas, they may prey on domestic livestock. This has negatively impacted tolerance for preservation and conservation efforts. When cats compete for human resources, many are killed in retaliation.

Even our sweet little lioness cub, Essie, was at risk from the humans who did not want her in their compound until she could be sent to sanctuary. They tried to take her and eliminate her. It was necessary, initially, to place a guard at her enclosure to keep her safe.

Poaching

Poaching is a tremendous threat to big cats and other species worldwide. The World Wildlife Federation cites a recent study showing that the targeted poaching of lions for their skin, teeth, claws, and bones accounts for 35% of known human-related lion killings. The statistics are very similar for tigers and other big cats.

Our beloved Phuku came from a facility where humans poisoned the lions and harvested their body parts. She had to endure horrific conditions and was trapped for quite some time before she was freed.

As David Gerber from Isindile explains, when you kill a lion, you are absolutely not killing just one cat.

Illegal Wildlife / Exotic Pet Trade

The illegal wildlife trade involves organized crime as well as individuals and other groups, which makes it even more challenging to eliminate. These individuals trap and send exotic wildlife into the United States and many other parts of the world, where there are willing buyers. Substantial numbers of big cats are sent to the Middle East, for example, where they suffer at the hands of their "owners." Most are tased regularly and subjected to other draconian measures to keep them under control.

Keeping big cats as pets is common in many parts of the world. It is very common in Israel, for example. Many Ukrainian and some Israeli nationals abandoned their cats, leaving them in cages to die or setting them loose on the streets. These cats have suffered tremendously and have been further traumatized and injured by shelling all around them.

Canned Hunting Facilities / Trophy Hunting

Also referred to as "shooting preserves," these are facilities where animals are trapped and confined within fenced enclosures and hunted. The hunting takes place at extremely close range and the kills are guaranteed. The animals don't stand a chance and also endure the trauma of seeing their fellow lions and knowing their fate.

As David Gerber from Isindile put it:

"When you poach or kill a lion, you never just kill one cat. If a trophy hunter shoots the dominant male lion, the effect is a vacuum, and other males will come in and take over the pride. To preserve their own genetic line, the first thing they do is kill the existing young clubs. So, shooting one male lion can result in the death of another ten to twelve lions."

Facilities Masquerading as Big Cat Sanctuaries / Unethical Sanctuaries

It is extremely common in South Africa for facilities posing as sanctuaries to use their cats for profit. There are a limited number of true sanctuaries, several of which are mentioned in this chapter.

Any sanctuary or other facility that allows you to hold and pet cubs, walk with big cats, or hosts events where humans are in close contact with the animals is exploiting them for profit.

As David Gerber from Isindile commented:

"We understand it from the perspective of human nature. A lion cub is a very cute little thing. There are people who will pay a lot of money to have their children sit and bottle-feed a lion cub. It's so easy to convince an average human to do this. Many don't want to hear what is the best thing for a lion's life. A cub should be sleeping twenty hours a day, and here they are being kept awake for twenty hours a day so humans can have them sit on their laps.

"There are many pseudo-sanctuaries that are open to the public. They have restaurants, bars, and cubs, and make a great deal of money. From our perspective as an ethical sanctuary, we really have got to convince the public not to support those places. You will pay a couple of hundred thousand rand. Far better to take that money and support an ethical sanctuary that is doing something to improve the lives of previously exploited big cats. These places are worse than a zoo because of the human interaction, which is not good for those animals, and they don't want that to be done to them."

Ethical sanctuaries never buy, sell, trade, or breed animals, and this should be clearly stated on their website. They generally are also not open to the public, although some may grant limited access for special groups.

Uncertain Future for South African Lions

South Africa has over 8,000 lions living in captivity, the largest captive lion population in the world. South Africa is finally taking steps that will protect some lions. The goal initially was for breeders and canned hunting facilities to shift into sanctuary models, but the current fate of those cats, as well as the cats at legitimate sanctuaries such as LLA and Isindile is currently uncertain. Unfortunately, there are already many organizations masquerading as sanctuaries, and it would take a tremendous amount of regulation and oversight to identify them and put them out of business.

Mountain Lions in the United States

While not technically considered to be big cats, mountain lions in the U.S. are under threat as well, and we include two interviews with our mountain lion friends in the U.S. They face similar challenges to their counterparts in other parts of the world, although they are not bred and harvested.

There are many who would like to eliminate them, and there have been a number of attempts to allow the killing of mountain lions for sport or to eliminate them to protect livestock. The truth is that while a mountain lion may feed on livestock, they are not a primary cause of livestock losses. Diseases, weather, and other factors are the primary risk factors.

It is rare for mountain lions to kill domestic pets, although it can and does occur. Typically, only ill, injured, or very elderly mountain lions prey on domestic pets. Mountain lions are shy animals that try to avoid contact with humans. Many mountain lions are killed on roads and at highway crossings. The Mountain Lion Foundation estimates that there are a maximum of 30,000 in the United States and that humans are responsible for the death of more than 3,000 mountain lions in the U.S. each and every year.

How to Help

Every human being has the power to make a difference. You have the power to make a difference. These beautiful, sacred beings need us now more than ever.

Educate Yourself

Educate yourself and others, and make your voice heard. The more people that know and understand their plight, the more hope there is for the big cats in the world. Follow sites that educate about the plight of the big cats. Post educational information on your social media to help others understand. Share the stories of animals who have suffered the consequences of human aggression against animals. Simply talking to folks can be very powerful. The more people who understand and object, the harder it will be to continue detrimental practices.

Advocate for Better Outcomes for Wildlife

Get political. Sign petitions and promote legislation and other initiatives in support of animals. As I referred to previously, America's own big cats, the mountain lions, are under attack and face many of the same threats in the U.S. as well.

Avoid Businesses and Facilities That Treat Animals Unethically

Stay away from visiting facilities that offer interactions with their animals (petting, etc.) or engaging in activities that negatively impact them. Boycott circuses or other entertainment venues that use wild animals.

Promote Responsible Tourism

Support eco-tourism initiatives that benefit local communities and wildlife conservation. Avoid travel to areas where wildlife is not respected.

Support Conservation and Anti-Poaching Efforts

Organizations like Born Free, the David Shepherd Wildlife Foundation, African Parks, the World Wildlife Fund, and the Lion Recovery Fund are actively working on conservation and anti-poaching efforts. They focus on habitat protection, research, community involvement, and reducing human-wildlife conflict.

If you are able to support these organizations financially, that's wonderful. Volunteering and being active on their social media pages is another way to support their efforts.

Support Ethical Big Cat Sanctuaries

If you are visiting a sanctuary, please turn off the location finder on your phone and avoid taking any photos or posting anything to social media that would give any clue as to the location of the sanctuary. Poachers use this information to illegally access sanctuaries, which can lead to devastating results. Many sanctuaries in the U.S. also purposely do not display their address for fear of harm to their animals and, in some of the horse sanctuaries I have volunteered at, for fear that former abusive owners will try to reclaim the horses they harmed or severely neglected.

As with any nonprofit, some are better than others, and there are absolutely many unethical organizations out there. You may sponsor the sanctuary in general, or, if you fall in love with one of the cats, you can sponsor them specifically. The following are several we can guarantee treat their cats with the love and respect they deserve:

Love Lions Alive (LLA)

We have worked with Andi and LLA for close to five years. The animals are well-fed, well cared for, and well loved. Andi understands lions better than anyone else on the planet, as far as we are concerned. It goes much deeper than basic care. It is a place where lions and other big cats are revered and honored and where their behavior is well understood. There are primarily lions at LLA, but there are also tigers, jaguars, and a mountain lion. To find out more or donate, visit lovelionsalive.org.za.

Isindile

We have worked with Ansa and David Gerber for several years and highly recommend them as well.

The cats are well taken care of, loved, respected, and honored. They have tremendous patience with new cats as they are acclimating, as does Andi. They, like Andi, are wonderful, amazing human beings who are doing tremendous good in the world. Isindile has some incredible tigers and lions, as well as our beloved leopard, Brave. To find out more or donate, visit https://www.isindilesanctuary.org.za/.

The Wild Animal Rescue Center

The Wild Animal Rescue Center, led by Natalia Popova and UAnimals, provides temporary shelter and medical treatment for animals in war zones. We have them to thank for rescuing a number of cats we have had the privilege of working with. This is who the soldiers call when they come across a cat abandoned by their humans and trapped in their cages. The animals in these zones are incredibly traumatized, and these folks are doing lifesaving work while their own lives have been traumatized and torn apart by war.

http://address-patreon.com/wildanimalsrescueua

Animal Defenders International

This is an amazing organization that supports big cats, other wildlife, and, from time to time, domestic animals. They care deeply, and their animals are treated beautifully. To find out more or donate, visit https://www.ad-international.org/adi_home. These folks literally risk their lives to bring these beautiful cats to safety.

AAP Primadomus

AAP is a facility based in Spain, Germany, and the Netherlands, rescuing primates and other exotic animals. There is absolutely a feline focus at AAP, and it is a wonderful organization doing excellent work. To find out more or donate, visit https://es.aap.eu/sobre-aap.

Ethical Sanctuaries in the U.S.

When it comes to ethical sanctuaries in the United States, while we are not familiar with all of them, there are several that we can recommend. To find additional sanctuaries worthy of your donations, you can also visit the Global Federation of Animal Sanctuaries website. They inspect and accredit sanctuaries. That said, there are lapses of time between inspections and reaccreditation. I strongly recommend doing some additional research to ensure these sanctuaries have credibility, and ask directly if they buy, sell, trade, or have interactive exhibits.

Performing Animal Welfare Society (PAWS)

This sanctuary is located in California. PAWS is dedicated to the protection of performing animals, to providing sanctuary for abused, abandoned, and retired captive wildlife, to the preservation of wild species and their habitats, and to promoting public education about captive wildlife issues. They are an advocacy agency in addition to providing lifelong care for the animals at their facility.

They have the following statement on the homepage of their website:

A true sanctuary, PAWS does not breed, buy, sell, or trade animals. We provide a permanent home and lifetime care tailored to the history and needs of each individual.

To find out more or donate, please visit www.pawsweb.org.

WildCat Ridge

This sanctuary is located in Oregon. They provide a safe, natural, lifetime home for captive-born wildcats in need. They primarily focus on wildcats, but they also care for hybrid cats, domestic feral cats, dogs, and a herd or flock of donkeys, cows, and roosters.

They have the following statement on the homepage of their website:

We are not open to the public and we do not buy, sell, breed, or exhibit our animals.

To find out more or donate, please visit wildcatridgesanctuary.org.

Use Your Own or Your Animals' Personal Power

If you pray, use affirmative prayer for a better world for the big cats and all wildlife. Send love. It is amazing how powerful the energy of love is. If you are aware of a facility or area in which big cats are suffering or treated poorly, focus on your heart and share the energy of love. They will absolutely feel it, and it can make a tremendous difference.

See with your Reiki eyes and understand that even the most bedraggled animal is whole in all of the ways that matter. Know that when you see their courage, their ability to heal, and their potential, you support them in making that a reality. If you are an energy worker, first seek the animal's permission before sharing energy and follow their lead.

You can partner with your animal companion in this. Let them know what you are doing and ask if they would like to send love as well. My animals have felt it is important to be involved, and I include them. One of the most important things we can do to support animals on the planet is to bring them together to support each other and build their collective strength and connection.

The most beautiful part of our planetary healing work has been observing groups of animals we have supported coming in to support other groups of animals. This includes beings most folks don't often think about. The insects are a powerful and loving group who frequently participate to support their larger non-human allies.

Understand Zoo Animals and Give Them the Respect They Deserve

As has been mentioned, many animals inhabiting zoos have made a deliberate choice to represent their species. They absolutely do not want our pity and thrive when we recognize their wholeness.

On a recent zoo trip, I thanked the various animals for their courage, their service to their own kind, and to the planet. The responses I received were extraordinary. There was a tremendous amount of emotion from each group on being seen and recognized for who they truly are. There were tears in my eyes, and they weren't mine. It makes a difference. The reaction from the crocodiles was the most profound. Many animals that humans vilify as monsters are negatively impacted by human perceptions.

The Interviews

Overview

All of the cats we interviewed have profound advice for humans, both with respect to healing the Earth and healing mankind in general. They also speak on a number of additional topics, including animals in captivity, their own personal trauma, the impacts of inbreeding, animals in Zoos and sanctuaries and the importance of apex predators. I initially intended to separate them by topic; however, each interview is multi-faceted and addresses multiple themes, so I have chosen to organize them by facility and species.

I have included a number of animals in spirit, as well as several zoo and sanctuary animals from the United States. While mountain lions are not officially classified as big cats, they are the largest cats in the U.S. and very near and dear to our hearts. My own beloved cat my wise, sweet Prince was interviewed at nine months of age for his perspective on bonding with your own animals.

As you read through the interviews, I encourage you to take their messages to heart and to deeply consider how to implement some of their suggestions into your own personal life. I guarantee you this powerful information will both touch your heart and support you in your own personal transformation.

Love Lions Alive[5]

The Lions

Rasta (Formerly known as Cecil)

Background:

Rasta came to Love Lions Alive Sanctuary from Ukraine after years of effort to rescue him. He had been living in dire conditions, in a barred cage, as an individual's "object." The Love Lions Alive team felt impassioned to take this lion out of his cage in Ukraine and give him a South African home and a life of dignity and health.

People who had witnessed Rasta in the cage warned us that he was an "abnormal" lion because he banged his head into the bars of his cage repeatedly. This, however, was in response to the life he was being made to live at the time. Since arriving at Love Lions Alive Sanctuary, he has become a grounded and calm lion who loves to stretch out in his new large space and in the African sun. He has come leaps and bounds from the distressed and sickly lion he once was.

---

[5] Background information from the LLA website, shared with permission.

Rasta is a gentle, dignified, awe-inspiring, and magnificent lion, whom we are honored to know and care for. At the moment, he is alone in his enclosure, but we are planning to move him in with Demira, Diya, and Frieda when he is strong enough. Rasta has healed tremendously, and this move will be coming in the very near future. The three "ladies" mentioned let Cathy and me know that they hold Rasta in very high regard, and all four are looking forward to their new life together.

Interview:

Humans have lost their capacity to love without reservation. So many have been so wounded and beaten down by other humans that they have lost the way back to their own hearts. There is much to be appreciated in the human race, and there is great potential.

Humans need to stop serving the god of money, possessions, and ownership. In the pride, we all work together for the good of all. There is no lack, scarcity, or competition. We are able to share and support each other at the highest levels. Even for those that we exclude from the pride, there is a loving aspect. The animal itself not the pride makes the decision to isolate.

Cooperation and collaboration are the way of the future, and the lack of it is the reason for man's downfall. Most humans are unable to be satisfied, always looking for something to change who they are or the way they feel. They must find their way back to their own hearts to be whole.

Rasta shared that when he first arrived, people looked at him as they do some others, and they saw his wounds. It made their hearts hurt. Humans don't want to see their own wounds, so they focus on the wounds of others.

What you do to the Earth and others, you do to yourselves. When you hurt, abuse, and kill us, you hurt your heart and your own soul. There is no separation between us. We are all one. When you destroy the Earth, you destroy yourselves. When you heal yourselves, you heal us all.

What the Earth needs most is for people to open their hearts, heal their own wounds and hearts, and reconnect to the whole. People avoid looking at their own wounds because it's hard, but what they don't realize is that it is very necessary and worthwhile.

We thank you for always listening to us, caring about us, and putting our words out there. This book is very important to us and will be life-changing. You are some of the few who have learned to see and acknowledge our wounds while understanding we are not our wounds. You see us for the essence our soul and that is more valuable than you can ever imagine.

Reign (Lioness)

Background:

Andi first met Reign when she was a tiny cub at a facility where she first became involved with lions. She was there to help a friend and was disturbed by the practices at the facility, but made a decision to stay to help the cats as best she could, with a goal of rescuing all that she could and bringing them under her loving care. Two of Reign's siblings were killed by a male lion as tiny cubs, and Andi rescued the remaining three.

Interview:

Beloveds, this is a very auspicious day. It is a rare privilege to have the opportunity to reach out to humankind. I come not with anger, but some of my words may seem stern, because it is necessary to communicate in this manner so humans will understand where I am coming from.

The human race is destroying itself. As others have said, when they destroy nature when they destroy animals they destroy themselves. It goes much deeper than that. The very hearts and souls of humanity are at stake. The species is losing its capacity to truly connect with the natural world. This must be addressed as quickly as possible. There will come a time when it will be very difficult to turn back.

All animals in all sanctuaries, particularly the cats, are there for a reason and are connected to each other. Each is critical to the whole. They are meant to be together to do their worldly work. This is why it was so critical that the cats we were separated from returned to LLA.

We work together for the good of all, as well as for our own species. We not only work to heal the animals in the sanctuaries, but we also work together to bring in love and support for the people who care for us, as well as working to heal the world. To heal the world, one must heal oneself first. As our wounds are healing, the wounds of the planet heal as well. The role of the sanctuary animals is very important.

Animals in zoos have a similar but different role. Some people do not like to see animals in captivity. There is controversy around this. They do not like to see animals taken away from their mothers and families.

The animals in zoos, for the most part, are ambassadors for their counterparts in the wild, but they are more than that. They are holding the energy and space for their counterparts in the wild as well. They are providing energetic support for those who are under threat.

And know that the animals in the wild are very much connected to the zoo animals. They are connected to the consciousness of their own species. When something happens to an animal in the wild, it energetically and emotionally affects the zoo animals of that species.

What happens to one dolphin affects all dolphins. What happens to one lion affects all lions. What happens to one giraffe affects all giraffes. We are all connected through the web of consciousness. Humans are connected in the same way.

What affects one affects all. What you do to one, you do to yourself and the world. When you are harming someone, you harm the entire human race. Humans must learn this to heal themselves and the world.

To support us, recognize our power and our vital role in creating change on the planet. We want people to be aware of the web of consciousness of different species and the fact that we are all connected. What affects one affects all. It is very important for humans to understand that, so that when they visit a zoo, they understand the bigger picture.

Odin

Background:

The Love Lions Alive team believes that Odin was born on September 7, 2016, as he was four days old when we were called on September 11 to take him in. Odin was born on a lion breeding farm, where he had been intended to be a cub that tourists could bottle-feed and, eventually, be killed for the lion bone trade. However, Odin was a small, sickly, and dehydrated cub that the farm didn't believe was worth the money and effort to nurse back to health.

Luckily for him, due to a tourist having the tenacity to find and reach out to us at Love Lions Alive, we had the opportunity to intervene. We collected him and his sister, Mulan, and bought the appropriate supplies from a veterinarian.

Odin was nursed back to health with Ringer's lactate, glucose, and antibiotics being administered to him. He was syringe-fed while getting stronger. Odin made a brave recovery and grew up alongside Mulan at our sanctuary. He has grown into a healthy and large lion our biggest lion even bigger than Taai and Shannon. Odin is an affectionate and gentle lion who can be gregarious in his playfulness. He spends most of his time lying on top of the boulders in his enclosure and is capable of some serious "chilling." He is also a very affectionate and loving cat. Odin was excited to share his perspective with us.

Interview:

When they hurt us, they hurt themselves. They do not realize the depth and interconnection between everything on the planet, but it goes much deeper than anyone realizes. It is the spiritual, the energetic connection that unites all life. It may appear that we live in a very physical world, but it is the energy that ties everything together. It's important that humans treasure and protect this.

The way humans cut themselves off from this universal force they are able to do the harmful things they do because they are disconnected from the web of life. Please understand that my well-being is your well-being. What touches the one touches the all. There is a way to bring the species together that can change what is happening in the world, but humans have to be willing to do that. We have the power to save the Earth, but it requires a willingness to approach things differently and have a different perspective. See other beings not as competition, but as a unified whole. Serving the whole serves each one.

Human hearts are shut down in order to enable them to live the life they are living. It is this disconnection that is the underlying force behind all health problems. Every human ailment comes from this.

Humans are destroying the animals, the planet, and their own souls by the actions they are taking. Human souls are suffering. We must heal our souls. People must open their hearts to themselves first then they can heal the world. We cannot heal the world until humans heal themselves. People must get more in touch with their own hearts and heal their own ego by this I mean profit, greed, and materialism in all its forms. It's time for humans to lead with their hearts, as the two of you have.

We need forgiveness. It starts with forgiving ourselves, then forgiving others. They must love themselves. They cannot learn to love others until they do. Humans must tend to their souls. They are so focused on the physical, which is only an illusion. The love is the truth.

The human race is somewhat at a crossroads, and if we do not do our healing work in this lifetime, the damage will be carried forward into the next. If you wish your children to have any kind of life worth living, hear these words. We are robbing our children of their birthright to be connected to all things.

I know this sounds very heavy and serious, but it's important for humans to lighten up. You take things way too seriously. Lighten up. Have some fun. Joy is what will heal the world. People need to bring more joy into their lives. The materialism is irrelevant not important. What's important is love and joy and getting in touch with your heart.

Umbhali

Background:

Umbhali came to Love Lions Alive Sanctuary after a veterinarian in Warden, South Africa, called us about an unwell cub from a breeding farm. The cub had collapsed due to pain and could not even raise his head. The breeding farm signed him over to the veterinarian to shoot, but the veterinarian instead contacted us. We collected the cub and took him to a specialist veterinarian for three weeks of treatment.

We named him "Umbhali," which means "he who tells the story." Umbhali tells a story of incredible tenacity and strength of character. He has come such a long way and has gained so much strength. He also tells the story, however, of the conditions lions are being kept in and we will continue to hope that his story is heard and sheds light on all of the cubs who did not make it out.

Umbhali has grown into a handsome, gentle, and angelic lion. He has the sweetest, softest personality. He does still show some signs of the lack of care he once received, such as "star-gazing." After many months of work, we have moved him in with Nahara. They live a loving life together.

Interview:

There is much to share, but I worry it will fall on deaf ears. Mankind has not developed the capacity to listen to the natural world and to act on what they know in their hearts is true. Man has become accustomed to being led, rather than thinking for themselves. Man has a tendency to go with whatever the masses are thinking, rather than to delve in and trust the messages they hear from their own hearts. This is unfortunate.

There is so much that could free the human race if they were able not only to open their hearts and listen but really hear what is being spoken. Not only in their minds, but in their hearts and their very souls. The time has come to pay deep attention to the animal kingdom.

There is a way to save the Earth and preserve the integrity of all its beings. But I'm afraid mankind is very hesitant to know about it because it will take some effort on their part. It might upset their view of the world, their perspective on themselves, and their beliefs about what mankind is currently all about.

I am an example of what it means to never give up and never give up hope. I was bred for the purpose of becoming a trophy for somebody's wall. I knew that was not my path. My heart and my soul knew that I had a bigger purpose.

I was in a bad place. I was not well taken care of. I was not cared about. I was seen as something to be tossed away or used to make money. I was not treated well, and because of this, my body was weak, in pain, and did not develop properly. And yet I knew there was more for me.[6]. They named me Umbahli, which means "he who tells the story," and I do wish for my story to be told.

---

[6] Umbahli was raised at a "farm" where inbreeding was the norm. When we first met Umbahli, he found it very difficult to ambulate and could

There are so many others like me who were not as fortunate, but I never gave up hope. I always stayed tuned to my heart, and I always stayed tuned to the light. By keeping my focus there, kind people found me. Kind people helped me escape. And, as you know, wonderful, wonderful people took me in.

They helped me heal my body and my spirit. They helped me have faith that there are good people in the world. I now live this beautiful life as a lion should. I live in a beautiful place with other wonderful lions all around me. A day does not go by that I am not thankful to be here.

I have a soulmate in Nahara. I have a little sister in Nahara. And all of the other lions here we are family. The people here are so kind and loving and determined to do what they can to make a better world for lions.

There are two things that I wish for people to know.

One, I wish for people to know how many others there are like me. I hear you speak about my nature and how I am sweet and gentle and kind and loving. I hear you say it, and I hear Andi say it. I love that you feel that way about me. However, I am not the only one. There are many others like me.

People need to be aware of what is happening with lions. And it's not just lions animals who are bred for the sole purpose of being

---

hardly move his body. He was destined for a canned hunting facility prior to being rescued.

killed. It must stop. So I do thank you two for giving me this opportunity to tell my story, and to get the stories out there about those who are not as fortunate as me and will not survive.

What you said about courage I want to talk about how important it was from Day One, when I arrived at the hospital and they didn't know if I was going to survive. I was in very bad shape. You all sent me healing, and I felt it. Andi and the others at LLA always believed I could get better, and the people at the hospital believed the same. I wish to acknowledge and reinforce that.

They saw my courage, my strength, and my spirit and that was what made the difference. That is why I am still here today.

I also wish to spread the message to always have hope, even when things seem at their darkest. Stay tuned into your heart. Stay tuned into the light. There is always hope for you, no matter what your circumstances are. And there is always hope for the world. As long as there are people who have compassion and are able to tune into their hearts (and there are many), there is always hope for the world.

The Tigress

Background:

Kanosha is a female tigress who was bought to be kept as a pet and companion to Igor, a male tiger with the same owner. She had been kept in a house in Gauteng, South Africa. Kanosha had been in relatively fair condition compared to some atrocities we have seen, but she was overweight and had high cholesterol. This was due to having had no exercise and an incorrect diet of frozen chicken pieces. A house is an inappropriate habitat for a Siberian tiger.

Kanosha's owner decided to give her and Igor to Love Lions Alive. Panthera Africa and Ban Animal Trading worked alongside us on the rescue.

Kanosha arrived at Love Lions Alive Sanctuary in May of 2021. She loves her new home and is making the most of the space she has to move around in, the boulders she has to climb, and the vegetation she can hide in. She is a gorgeous tigress, and Love Lions Alive strives every day to fulfill the honor of caring for her and giving her the best life we possibly can.

Igor and Kanosha were the first cats that we spoke with on our journey with LLA.

Interview

Humanity needs to wake up. When they destroy the planet, they destroy themselves. I have never witnessed a species so hell-bent on self-destruction. Humans have lost touch with their hearts. They feel separate. It is the sense of separation that is at the root of all human evil.

They want power over instead of sharing power with the collective whole. Humans fight more against each other than they fight for each other. This must change. I am aware of the wars. I am aware of the current Israel–Hamas conflict, as well as the United States' involvement in this.

This is not the way. If all countries would put down their arms, go into their hearts, and be reconnected with what it is to love to love themselves, to love others then the world would be a beautiful place.

If humans decided to love and support each other instead of fighting with each other, what a beautiful world this would be. There is still time for the planet to rebound, but that time is limited. Please, humans, take this message to heart and know that I speak the truth.

I have been on this planet since the beginning, in many forms. I have been in human form, so I can speak plainly about this and with the perspective of having been a human. I was killed in a war. My family was brutalized. I carry this sadness with me from lifetime to lifetime.

Take it from one who has been on this Earth for millennia the way to healing is love.

The Jaguars Speak

Background:

Amazon is a strong, capable, and feisty female jaguar who came to Love Lions Alive Sanctuary in March of 2020. Amazon has three legs. She and her daughter, Brazil, came to us after a zoo in Bloemfontein, South Africa, was shut down for its lack of animal welfare standards. The Society for the Prevention of Cruelty to

Animals (SPCA) and the Department of Environmental Affairs reached out to us to give the mother-daughter duo a new, safe home.

When the Love Lions Alive team went to collect Amazon, she was hissing and snarling in fear, occasionally lunging at the iron bars. Now, she and her daughter live peacefully in the enclosure we built specifically for them at the sanctuary.

We really wanted to give them a life that satisfies their natural jaguar instincts, and their enclosure has a dam, wetlands, reed beds, rocks, and long grass.

Amazon has taken to her new home with confidence and glee, making the most of the water, reeds, and hiding spots. She is no longer fearful, but self-assured and confident. She loves to emerge from her hiding spots when we are near her fence and is extremely curious. She will live out the rest of her life at Love Lions Alive Sanctuary with her beloved daughter, Brazil, and we will continue to cherish every minute of it.

It is important to note that the jaguar is considered a very magical animal in Mesoamerican culture. It represents strength, power, and leadership, often associated with gods and rulers. It also symbolizes the ability to transition between worlds, both physically and spiritually. Jaguars are considered agents of transformation and vision.

The destruction of the Amazon rainforest is a major threat to these sacred beings, and Amazon and Brazil have asked Cathy and me to work on this. We have found Amazon and Brazil to be very magical cats and will be delving deeper into jaguar magic. They have expressed a desire to share their teachings with us, which may become the subject of another book.

Interview:

Amazon and Brazil began by sharing their insights into the magic of jaguars. Jaguars are power animals who have been in relationship with shamans and other highly evolved humans throughout the ages. Because of our culture, we are very connected with the ancient ways and the indigenous ways of being. This is the way to live in true partnership with the Earth.

The indigenous people walk in harmony with and lightly upon the Earth. These individuals and communities live in collaboration and harmony with the natural world something that is gravely lacking in the U.S. and other industrialized nations. They struggle with the way humans are currently treating the Earth, the Earth's creatures, and each other. People have lost their souls and their own medicine, and that desperately needs to be reclaimed.

The human race has great potential if they choose to open their hearts and live in a way that benefits and does as little harm as possible to the other creatures of the Earth. It would benefit humans greatly to learn from all animal species how to survive and how to take care of yourselves, each other, and the planet.

Learn from the predator-type cat species, the wolves, and the coyotes, because the predator carnivores know how to take care of themselves and their offspring while still living in harmony and balance with themselves and with nature.

The human race is out of balance. If we had one thing to say to humans, it would be to reconnect to your soul and with the natural world. To do so, spend time in nature. Connect with the animals. Be still and listen to what the animals have to share. All you have to do is be still and open your heart. They have much wisdom.

If you do that, it will help humans reconnect with their souls, spirit, and their own truth and wisdom. Contrary to popular belief, humans have access to a great deal of wisdom and knowledge, but they have lost this connection because they have become so caught up in greed, power, and materialism. They have lost touch with the sacred.

You could not imagine what a beautiful place this would be if humans were in touch with their ancestors and this sacred knowledge and wisdom. If they were to regain the connection with their own souls, their own hearts, and the ancient wisdom, this would be a much better place.

Each person who wants to see a better world needs to know it starts with you as an individual. Heal your own heart, your own soul, and get back in touch with the ancestors, the ancient wisdom, the ancient knowledge, and the animals. There are many humans who long to do this, yet they don't understand where or how to start. It doesn't matter how you start just start.

Follow your intention and lead with your heart. If your heart tells you to go sit in a park, sit in a park. If you are drawn to read a certain book, then read it. Just be open. Open your heart, open your mind, and let it come to you.

As Cindie has spoken of elsewhere in the book, it is truly your intent your deepest intent that matters: to connect with the natural world, to see others, all others, as a mirror of yourself and your own experience, and to change your way of being in the world.

You have everything that you need. It is desire, followed by positive actions, that will create the shift. We are not talking about anything heroic. You don't have to sell all your possessions and go live in an igloo.

Every living being is sacred. There is a holiness about each and every species and every individual within every species. Those who commit crimes, who are destructive and unkind, have shadows over their hearts. The disconnection between humans and heart is vast. They have been led to believe other things are so much more important.

We are telling you the opposite. If you disconnect from your head and move into your heart, everything you have ever wished for will fall into place. What you will find is that many of the things you once wished for like a beautiful house and a new car are not what you truly wish for, but something a million times better.

Understanding the state of true happiness and what leads to it is something the human race needs to better understand. Look to those who walk softly upon the Earth as an example for mankind to follow. Set aside your anger, your disappointment, your hurt that the world is not what you would wish it to be. Visualize instead the world that you would like to see, and focus on that.

Isindile

The Tigers Speak

Yehudah

Background: Yehudah was bought from a breeder in Pakistan and kept as a pet. However, after only a few weeks, his "owner" surrendered him to a veterinarian because he was in great pain, unable to walk, and virtually paralyzed. It was discovered that he was suffering from multiple bone fractures as a result of poor nutrition.

He received the required veterinary care and underwent a long period of rehabilitation while in the care of the Islamabad Wildlife Management Board. He had to learn to walk again, but typical of him, nothing could break this young cub's spirit. Once fully recovered, he was relocated to Isindile in collaboration with IWMB, The Aspinall Foundation, and Second Chance Wildlife Pakistan.

Yehudah was released into Or's enclosure on Valentine's Day 2024, but he was definitely not Queen Amber's (his direct neighbor) Valentine! Amber was not happy with this young and extremely playful tiger living next to her. Although she would growl and snarl at him every time she saw him, his gentle personality allowed him to take it in stride, and he never seemed offended by her attitude.

Yehudah was named in memory of Amber and Or's brother, Judah, whose death at Seaview Predator Park was the catalyst for bringing Amber and Or to Isindile. Yehudah, along with Sahara, is their most active big cat.

Cathy and I have found Yehudah to be a charming and delightful cat. He is over the moon living at Isindile and is most frequently jovial and in excellent spirits.

Interview:

Beloveds,

It is a very happy day in my life. It is my joy to do whatever I can to make a difference in the world for my kind. I have been so blessed with a beautiful life. My heart is filled with love and gratitude towards these beautiful people and towards you, the lovely ladies who have helped us all heal, recover, and regain our tiger natures.

I want humans to know that they *can* connect with animals, just as the two of you do. If you love tigers, or lions, or whales, or gorillas and if you want to help them thinking about them, sending them love, feeling them in your heart, and connecting with them in this way, whether it is one individual or an entire species, *will* make a difference.

This will heal the animals and yourself.

You do not have to be an animal communicator to do this. It is valuable, critically important, and makes a tremendous difference—just feeling love in your heart for them. It will heal their hearts and yours. This is very much needed.

Do *not* go into the trauma of their circumstances. This does not serve.

Amber and Or (Interviewed in Spirit)

Background:

Amber and Or were our first-ever rescues, and the day they arrived, ISINDILE was officially born and became a reality. They were rescued from the notorious Seaview Predator Park outside of Port Elizabeth when it finally closed down.

Although Amber and Or were blood sisters, they lived in separate enclosures, and we were told that they hated each other. Or always lived alone, but Amber had a male partner called Judah. His untimely death at the hands of another tiger was the catalyst for relocating all the big cats from the facility. Judah's death was not in vain.

Initially, Amber and Or could not find a new home and were the last two big cats left at the facility. We were told that the fact they lived alone and could not be socialized had made them an unpopular choice for rehoming. David and Ansa strongly believed that their previous environment had contributed to their dislike for each other and that, under the right circumstances, they could be integrated in the future. As such, they built their enclosures with a shared fence and gate in the hope that one day they could open it and allow them to be together.

Unfortunately, fate had other plans. After only three months at Isindile, Or was diagnosed with advanced liver cancer and had to be laid to rest. In that time, Amber and Or would often lie at the fence together, communicating with each other. David and Ansa never detected any signs of aggression and remain convinced that, had Or lived longer, they would have happily shared an enclosure together.

We found comfort in the knowledge that Or was still with us in spirit, guarding over Isindile. Or became the Spirit of Isindile.

After Or's passing, Amber was the only big cat at Isindile, and she craved their company. Every morning when they went up to visit her, she was already waiting for them. The three of them would spend hours walking along her fence line or quietly sitting together, surrounded by the beauty and tranquility of nature.

Amber loved lying at the top of her enclosure, staring into the distance with a look that gave the impression of ownership. It was this attitude that resulted in her becoming the Queen of Isindile, a title she carried with distinction.

Amber was an extremely vocal tiger and continually surprised us with new sounds. She had the most beautiful way of humming quietly as we walked around her enclosure and groaning as she rolled back and forth in the grass.

Cathy and I knew Or only briefly, but had many lovely encounters with Amber. She was indeed regal and is greatly missed.

Interview:

The world has lost its way. As you have heard from many of the other cats, when humans harm us, they harm themselves. It is time for humanity to lay down their arms. The whole world is at stake. The violence and hatred are becoming stronger and stronger. The animals of the Earth feel this deeply within their bones. They understand everything that is happening. They wish to be of service to mankind.

That is why we all have come. This is a planet that was faltering. We were needed to support those who walked upon the Earth. We came with love in our hearts, with the deepest intent to serve, to be of service, to make a difference for mankind yet we were treated with contempt and absolute cruelty more often than we wish to remember.

Mankind does not always recognize the difference between what is good and what is expedient. There is so much fear in the hearts of men now. The human race is at risk. We have done all we can. Our numbers are dwindling. Our species has been hated and hunted almost to extinction.

It is critical and imperative that people know that the number of tigers is dwindling to such an extent, and the diversity in their gene pool is at such risk, that it is almost too late to turn back the clock. So we share this message with some urgency.

We have been very disappointed in mankind, but knowing there are those like Ansa and David, Andi Rive, and you and Cathy gives us hope that it is not too late. We speak with urgency because the situation is indeed dire and urgent.

We ask for mankind to open their hearts. It is only those whose hearts are shut down and dead inside that are able to do what they do to us. Because, as so many have said, what they do to us they do to themselves.

Mankind does not always know when a good thing is looking them straight in the face. They are too anxious to make money, get home to their loved ones, rest, have a drink at night, and disengage themselves from their daily life. This is not the way. There is more isolation in this.

It is the connection that humans crave. However, many humans are not wise enough to realize this.

There is still time to rebuild the connection. When mankind sees us as we truly are as helpers and showers of the way they must cease to try to eliminate us. We are killed for our body parts. We are killed for sport. We are killed because human beings want to feel strong and superior to us. Those are the humans who are least likely to engage in anything meaningful.

We believe we have said enough. We urge mankind to open their hearts, to get involved, to really think about what they are doing before they act. To not become so focused on the material world and their own problems that they cannot feel love inside their hearts.

We are here to love them, to support them, if only they will open their hearts to us.

God bless you for translating this message. It is very important. Please give our love to David and Ansa. We look down on you, our sweethearts. We love you every day, just as when we were with you. Your hearts and ours are linked for all time. There is no separation between us. We are truly as one.

God bless you for your gigantic hearts, your pocketbooks, and the way in which you approach the animals. Your respect is exquisite much appreciated and needs to be replicated. God bless you both.

I know you miss seeing us in our earthly forms, but we are still there. Amber is still the Queen of Isindile, and we both watch over you with great love and affection.

The Leopard Speaks

Brave

Background:

In December 2022, Brave was rescued by military volunteers during the war in Ukraine after his "owners" had fled the country. He had been kept as a pet at a private residence, with access to only 50m² of space. When the military volunteers found Brave, he was severely dehydrated and starved.

He was taken to the Wild Animal Rescue Center, where he received necessary veterinary care and spent some time recovering.

In November 2023, Brave was relocated to AAP Primadomus in Spain, where he received further veterinary care and behavioral rehabilitation.

In February 2024, after seeing footage of Brave, David and Ansa immediately felt a very strong spiritual connection to him. They reached out to AAP Primadomus/Stichting AAP to offer Brave a forever home at Isindile.

Brave arrived at Oliver Tambo Airport, Johannesburg, on February 6, 2025, where they met him and transported him home. During those first few days, he would only come out after sunset to take his food and explore his enclosure.

The name "Brave" definitely suits this stunning leopard.

Brave has been a major cheerleader and inspiration with respect to this book.

For a number of weeks, he kept Cathy up at night sharing his ideas and urging us to get moving!

Interview:

This book will change the way humans look at animals forever. My message is taking that a step further with all humans on the planet. Humans have lost touch with their soul, their connection to the planet, and with the entire concept that we are all one and part of the whole.

It is imperative that the human race on both an individual and collective basis slow down. People need to take time to connect with the Earth and their own hearts and souls. It is the separation that causes so much pain. More being, less doing.

This is not a new concept or idea, but people do not seem to be getting the message, so I am saying it again. If even a small percentage of humans would take a few moments each day to just sit quietly and be, and connect with their own hearts, the world would change drastically. It is so simple.

There is nothing to *do.* Just *be.* Humans have a very hard time doing that. Look at the animals as an example especially the big cats. We spend a large percentage of our time just being, connecting with the Earth and each other, and yet we have all that we need.

As you two know, even those of us who have been through a lot and have had rough times are able to connect with our peace. We are able to feel and be at peace. The healing power of *being* is vastly underrecognized.

I have much more that I could teach humans. You all have a lot to learn, but for now, this is my message: if you want peace within yourselves and within the planet, just *be.* Slow down and *be.* And for heaven's sake, stop worrying so much!

Spend more time being present and in the moment, where all of the wonder and healing resides. Humans spend too much time in the past and future, and all that truly exists resides in the present moment. This is not a new concept either, but people do not seem to understand or live by it.

For people who have animals, pay attention to them if you want to master the art of *being* and being in the present moment. Let your animals teach and guide you. Sit with them. They will show you.

If you do not have animals, observe the animals or birds or squirrels in your neighborhood. Squirrels are an excellent example. They always seem to be scurrying but are actually totally focused on the present.

Humans wonder how animals who have experienced suffering, abuse, and trauma can heal. This is possible because they are in the present moment, and in the present moment, they are safe. They don't need to carry the past with them.

Humans are causing our habitat destruction. They are destroying the planet not all humans, and most likely not the people reading this book. People see animals as objects to be used, profited from, or exploited for entertainment.

We're drawn to you, Cindie and Cathy, because you see us as individual, sentient beings, as many do. But the difference is that you recognize our wisdom, and you honor that and are open to learning from us. You don't place yourselves above us, and that is recognized and appreciated.

If more people would pay attention to the wisdom of animals, the world would be a better place.

Humans have gotten so far off course. They need to start making better choices and choose different ways of *being* if they want to save themselves, the planet, and the animals as well.

We thanked Brave. He made a little bow and walked away.

The Perspective of a Domestic Cat

Background:

Prince is an American Domestic Shorthair. I adopted him and his sister, Angel, from a large mixed litter of 15 barn cats in September of 2024. He is incredibly wise and loving, and soon after he came, he shared the following with me:

"Humans seem to have difficulty with relationships, but you and Todd (my husband) seem to have it mastered."

He was nine months old at the time of his interview and, as of this writing, is close to a year old. I included Prince's perspective to support humans in bonding with their own felines and to recognize the deep wisdom that they hold.

Interview:

You will be amazed that I am even wiser than you already imagine. I would like you to know that the smaller cats are very wise and evolved souls as much as the bigger cats, of whom you are so fond.

We have a special understanding and importance because we live directly with humans and influence their behavior. We understand more about who humans really are.

I would like to talk about how humans can bond with their own animals immediately. It is one of the more important things I have to discuss.

Most humans do not understand that they are not superior to animals. That is the biggest fallacy they make. They think they know what animals want, but most of them do not truly understand.

They need to get to know their pets and, ideally, learn how to speak with them like you do, so they can make sure everything is going okay and truly meet their pet's needs. I am grateful that you can do this. Maybe others can make an appointment with someone who can. It has been very helpful.

People must learn to be present, quiet, and still and just simply be with their animals. They need to slow down. Just be, with no expectations.

Your cats are here to heal you. Do not underestimate the value of cats. Dogs can be very fun and playful, and humans seem to enjoy that. However, there is a depth and a wisdom to our species that, while not lacking in dogs, is much more profound.

People undervalue cats and their importance in the world. In reality, we are the least aloof of all animals. We have our own ways, but we love deeply, we have great wisdom, and we are always looking to better the lives of our humans.

This is not to say that we are better than dogs just different. And also, that we should be valued more highly for what we bring to our relationships with humans.

The cat way is the softer way, and that is how humans should live their lives: in peace, in harmony with nature, and connected heart to heart with all living things. This is the only true path to happiness and the way that we should all live.

Cindie is making great progress in this area. She has farther to go; however, I believe that Angel and I are getting her there.

I am very proud to be a part of this book, and I encourage you to make haste. The sooner it comes, the better you will be able to protect all cats especially the lions in South Africa who are now at increased risk.

This is not to put pressure on you in any way. This is only to say: the sooner, the better.

Wild Animals

Background:

Tekoomse is a formerly wild Mountain Lion, who is now in spirit. His personal situation was a factor in the creation of wildlife crossings in the United States. We are all deeply indebted to this beautiful being, whose legacy will lead to a significant decline in wildlife deaths on freeways and major thoroughfares in the U.S.

Interview:

I was fortunate to live in a place where people care about wildlife and respect the mountain lion. I would like to thank those humans for all the love and care, especially in my final days. I felt the love they sent me during this time. This meant a lot to me.

I want people to know that all animals, including those in captivity or in the wild, do feel people's energy directed toward them. If they are sending us love, we do feel it, and it makes a tremendous difference. For those people who hate us, we feel this too.

We wish no harm to the humans or animals around us. We just want to live in peace. We are an important part of the ecosystem. Without us and other apex predators like wolves when we are killed off or starved and our numbers decline the natural balance is thrown off.

The killings are typically for human greed, entertainment, or simply for profit. People need to learn to respect all wildlife and allow nature to keep itself in balance. Although we are often vilified in the press or on social media, we are genuinely a gentle species. We hunt only to survive and nourish our physical bodies. We choose only those animals that are not well or are compromised in some way.[7]

---

[7] Animals are more attuned to the health status of other beings than humans are and are able to pick up issues with the body prior to a

This is according to the law of mutual cooperation and collaboration with all species. We respect all life, including the humans who have treated us with such contempt and hatred. Although many humans wish us harm, we hold them in our hearts and wish only good for all of them. We wish for the hearts and minds of humans to be healed so that they can look at the world with kind and compassionate eyes and hearts.

I am honored to feel that I had a small part in changing people's perceptions of who we are and what we are all about. We eagerly await the days when humans have a different perspective on us and we can live side by side in peace, each honoring the other. We do honor and respect mankind. When people glorify our killing, it is because their hearts and souls are wounded. It is not that humans should pity us, but we understand that is the place from which humans who kill for pleasure come. We have compassion for those individuals.

Zoo Animals*Background: Male and female Mountain Lions at an unnamed United States zoo. Their names are not provided for their own protection.*

Interview: When you go to a zoo, please do not look at us with pity, but as Cindie and Cathy do. This is one reason why it means so much to us when they visit. They see our magnificence beyond our

---

human awareness of an issue. Animals also have a tendency to hide illness from their humans so humans are not always aware until their conditions have progressed until they become more symptomatic

situation, and we appreciate that and wish others would have a similar perspective.

The mountain lions in America are under threat. We are in grave danger. Our numbers are dwindling. Humans do not realize the impact of the taking of our lands. It has been very frightening to us of late, because there have been many attempts to pass legislation to harm and kill us for no other reason than fear about something that might potentially happen.

God bless the two of you for all you do and the mountain lions that you have already supported. If you are open to this, we may, from time to time, point out cats that need your assistance.

Cindie, as you so often speak of, Americans do not realize the fiasco that will result if apex predators are eliminated or excluded from ecosystems. They only think of immediate needs. They do not have a perspective that supports planning with consciousness for the future.

It is time for them to take stock, to realize the service that we do for the United States of America. Life would be different without us. Deer would be overpopulated and vegetation would be destroyed. Animals we prey on, not simply for food, but when we are clear that their time on Earth is limited and they need support going home, will continue to suffer without our support.

We know and understand how much you love us. Please tell United States citizens that we are not to be feared. We are a force for good, although we understand it is difficult for them to understand our ways. We are hopeful that humans will read this book and take stock, and realize that we are a national treasure, not a national monster. We have a lot to offer.

Cougar energy is very powerful. If people would learn to see us in that way our power and spiritual medicine rather than looking at us as evil, something to be destroyed, and a threat, if they could see our magnificence, their lives would be transformed. If they begin to reconnect with animal life forms, they will save both themselves and this beautiful planet that has been provided for us.

Leopard Consciousness

Background: Male Black Leopard. This beautiful cat channeled information from the broader Leopard consciousness, rather than his own personal message.

Interview:

Humans need to understand that their days upon the planet are limited if they are not able to change their ways. The answer to everything is love. This begins with love for yourselves. Many humans despise themselves and feel they are less than. They take the cruel words spoken to them as children to heart and hesitate to release them so they can truly be free.

There are powers in the universe that are more powerful than the human mind can contemplate. However, humans have been given free will. They have access to wisdom that can change the world, but they must desire it.

If you wish to be an agent of change, open your heart to hear the messages and listen carefully. Do not take offense at what we are trying to say. Our only goal is to be of service to the human race. This is why we have come.

When we say things that may be difficult for you to hear, please understand this is not a criticism. It is an opportunity for your own personal healing. Open your hearts to all that is alive, to all that truly matters, instead of being a slave to money and possessions. Your hearts will heal. The difficulty in your life will disappear. When you are living from your heart, your life will be transformed.

It can be frightening at first to look deep inside yourselves because you carry so much trauma, and you seem to carry it with you from lifetime to lifetime. Humans think this is hard to do because they are so used to being in their minds, being up in their heads, that it is not comfortable for them.

The cumulative effect is a fear of trusting your own heart, fear of loving, fear of being open, and fear of being nothing without the trappings that the human race seems to find so magnificent. To open your heart is to truly be alive. There are just a small minority of humans who live this way. I urge you to become one of them. Set your fear aside. Open your hearts and you will be made whole.

If the human race is able to open their hearts, what a beautiful planet we would live in. If humans would connect with the joy and beauty of who they truly are, instead of who they have been molded to be, the world will heal and all will be well.

Start slowly. Take time every day to just sit, even for just a moment, and feel into your heart. Think about someone or something you love and feel it in your heart, whether it is a child, one of your animals at home, a flower, an ocean, or a river. Feel the love and start feeling into your heart. Then do a little more and a little more.

Many people have a unique opportunity to go to the zoo and sit with a lion, a big cat, an elephant, a rhinoceros. Even those who see us with love, compassion, and respect do not tune into our wisdom and our spirits. You can do this at the zoo. Pick an animal, sit with them. Feel their energy and their spirit and be open to the wisdom they have to share. Be open to what we have to share with you.

I guarantee you that if you do this, you will feel it and hear it. You can continue to connect with that animal in your quiet time. You will learn that you do not need to be physically present with us. Imagine us and feel us. If you are unable to go to a zoo or sanctuary, go to a park. There are squirrels. There are birds. Every living being has that wisdom and that spirit. Humans would be very wise to do so. Listen to them, hear them, and your life will be transformed.

People need to come to the zoo with a different perspective. We prefer to be seen for our greatness. There may be four walls surrounding us, but we are not contained by this. There is a part of us that is able to travel outside our dreary existence to connect with the higher realms. There are those from above who guide us. They have great wisdom, and they are wonderful teachers.

Snow Leopard Consciousness

Background: Male Snow Leopard. This beautiful cat channeled information from the broader Snow Leopard consciousness, rather than his own personal message.

Interview:

We were initially hesitant to speak to the human race because we were afraid our words would fall on deaf ears. Our species, because of our remote locations and inaccessibility, has not suffered as much as others of our kind. However, we feel, know, and understand the pain of our brothers and sisters, and it affects us deeply.

Those of us in captivity are in a unique position to bring awareness to our counterparts in the wild. A life in captivity is not a life for any animal. However, it is the reality, and most of us in captivity do see it as an opportunity to help people feel a connection with animals and hopefully feel love, respect, and compassion toward all animals.

We hope that by visiting with us, we can touch people's hearts and motivate them to do their part to make this world a better place for all animals. The big cats of the world are in danger all over the globe from hunting, poaching, habitat loss, environmental destruction, and human destruction. We wish for people to be aware of that.

When you come to a zoo and see the beautiful animals the lions, the tigers, the snow leopards, the rhinos, the smaller animals, the gorillas, the chimpanzees, the turtles remember that we are meant to live in the wild. We are meant to live on a healthy planet. We are meant to live in peace with those of our kind. Humans are the ones destroying this. Humans are the only ones who can change it.

As others have told you, we remain connected spiritually and energetically with our counterparts in the wild. That helps those of us in captivity stay connected to our wild roots. Hopefully, it helps those in the wild because we can raise awareness of the plight of our counterparts, so it is somewhat of a symbiotic relationship that helps all.

Having said that, what affects one affects all. As our counterparts in the wild suffer, we suffer.

We do not wish to tell people not to visit zoos, but we wish to tell people that in a perfect world, there would be no need for zoos and sanctuaries. The inhabitants of the planet would be taken care of and allowed to live in peace, beauty, and connection with nature. This applies to humans as well.

Humans just need to stop fighting with each other and attacking each other. It is long past time for wars to stop. When people kill each other, they kill not only other people they kill animals, the planet, and themselves. The killing must stop. The hatred must stop. The violence must stop.

It is time for humans to reconnect with their hearts and their spirits, and feel compassion for themselves and for each other. The human race is so deeply wounded. This is where it all comes from: all of the anger, all of the judgment, all of the fear, all of the violence these all come from the soul wounds that have been inflicted on humans and by humans.

Humans must heal and tend to their soul wounds. This is the only way the planet will begin to heal. They must listen to their hearts and their spirits, and rekindle their compassion first for themselves, then for others. People must learn to love themselves again. The hatred of others begins with the hatred of self, and it all comes from fear. They fear what they do not know, what they do not understand.

Humans who hate are really afraid, and it starts with fear of themselves. It is time to let go of fear and anger and choose love. Always choose love.

There is much hope in the animal kingdom for what will come to pass when humans change their hearts and minds through your beautiful writing and our sacred words.

The Inspiration

Andi's Story

When I first became involved, I didn't even have enough money to buy a cup of coffee let alone start a lion sanctuary. I am a facilitator and have faith that I am being used for this purpose. (Cathy and I clearly believe that Andi has been chosen.)

I got into this quite unexpectedly. I had no plans whatsoever to be involved. I was not aware of lion issues, what lion businesses in South Africa were involved in, or that lions were being bred on farms. I felt no specific alignment with lions. Even the fact that I was born a Leo, with my sun in Leo, moon in Leo, and Leo rising I would almost downplay anything about a lion connection, because aligning myself with lions seemed such an obvious choice. And I am not mainstream.

My first boyfriend was all about lions. Everything was about lions, and I painted, sculpted, and drew lions for his birthdays. Everything I did for him was about lions, but I did not admit or acknowledge a connection to them.

My involvement came quite by accident. My work involved house and shop renovations and décor for functions. I had a client whose home I was totally remodeling, and she ended up becoming a good friend. This was 2007. I went to visit her in 2011 when she had a brand-new baby. She was distressed about her father being in the hospital following a mental breakdown. He had a farm in the Free State. The farm was running unattended, and she was not sure what she could do to support him.

I offered to help. I had a gap in my work coming up, and school holidays were approaching as well. I was not familiar with the Free State. Later, when she informed me that the farm was a lion farm, the fact went straight over my head because I could not grasp the concept of a lion farm.

Off I went with my friend Kathy, and my children Shanéad and Rhoan, to the Free State to look at the farm and figure out what was going on. By the time we got there, my friend's father had been released from the hospital and was temporarily back at the farm.

We had to drive through a lion enclosure to get onto the farm. There were four large males in the enclosure we drove through, and they came and plastered their heads up against our car windows. Kathy was very nervous about this, and the children were clinging together in the middle of the seat. At that time, I didn't realize this was not something lions normally did. They literally pushed and walked us through a drive of about 600 feet.

As it was already dark, I didn't see any other lions that night only shining eyes reflected in the car lights. We went to sleep in a cottage, and around four a.m., the lions started roaring. There were 83 lions surrounding the house in all directions. The only way I can explain the feeling that came over me is to say it felt as if I had been switched on activated. As I listened to them roar, I realized this was why I was on Earth.

As the sun rose, I stood at the window, waiting to see the lions who had so moved my soul during the pre-dawn roaring. I had no idea what was waiting for me. As the sun rose over the mountain, I could see rows of fences and wiring, and lion shapes walking up and down, pacing. My heart plummeted, and I thought, *What was I doing there?* followed by the thought, *What were they doing there?*

It was in that moment that I realized I couldn't leave them there. I couldn't get in my car and drive away. I decided to stick it out. The following morning, I met Thulane, the lion manager. I took my notebook and pen and walked around the perimeter of the enclosures. I wrote down every name, the groupings the lions were in, and how they were related. I asked for Thulane's opinion on the personalities of the various cats. I took detailed notes.

Late that night, when everyone else was asleep, I studied my notes, committing the names to memory. The following day at 5 a.m., I met Thulane again. As we walked around the enclosures, I began to comment on what I was observing with the cats, calling each by name. I pointed out a lioness who was limping and another who was lying in the same spot as the day before. Thulane seemed shocked that I knew their names.

The importance of learning their names was that I no longer saw them as generic lions they became individuals to me.

There was an incident with one lioness that prompted me to call a veterinarian for support. I was told there was no veterinarian, which came as a bit of a shock because there were 83 lions on the property. The farm had been operating for nine years without one.

I called my friend, and she let me know that they did not have funds for a vet, but her father would humanely euthanize a lion when there was an issue.

There was a shed where the lions were skinned and a vat in which the lions were boiled for their bones and fat. I was determined to get a vet, even though I hadn't even had the money to make the trip to the farm in the first place. My friend Kathy had funded the trip, and she offered to pay for the vet.

This changed everything for me. Darting the lioness and being able to feel her body, teeth, and claws all plunged me into the world of not being able to turn my back on the lions. When the lioness woke up, she was still sleepy. She leopard-crawled toward me, mewling. By the end of my two weeks there, I was unable to leave this issue alone.

The situation, as I found it on the farm, was that my friend's father had a judgment against him amounting to several million rand, and the land plus all the animals on the farm, the lions and other wildlife included were to be auctioned to pay his debt five months later.

He had suffered a mental breakdown and was taken to a mental hospital, and I had his phone so I could look after things. Hunters and lion breeders were contacting me, asking about the lions so they could decide which ones they wanted to buy at auction.

It hit me like a ton of bricks. Not only did I need money to get the electricity back on for the lions and to fix a pickup truck (bakkie) that was not functioning to keep things running—I also needed to stay and get everything working. Most importantly, I had to keep the lions from going to auction in five months' time.

It became such a high priority to me that nothing else in the world seemed important anymore compared to the lives of those lions on the farm. I had a life back in the Cape, including my home and garden, pregnant clients for whom I would deliver babies, clients whose homes I was renovating, children in school, a deep love for karate, an ex-husband I co-parented with, and my own animals that I loved. Now all of that was teetering on one side of the scale, and the lions on the other. What was I to do?

My middle daughter, Shanéad, and I drove back and forth from the Cape to the farm a number of times over the next two months because someone had to run the farm. It was a 14-hour drive one way.

That's how it all started.

Breeding farms breed lions to sell, and lions breed at a prolific rate. A lioness has, on average, three cubs per litter. When her cubs are removed, she will cycle again within days and conceive again. Gestation is about 118 days. Lion farmers take the cubs away, thus forcing three pregnancies per year. If they have 30 breeding lionesses, they could have 270 to 300 cubs born per year.

The farmers do not keep the cubs. They breed to sell, otherwise there is a bottleneck effect. Looking back, I can see that I disrupted my friend's father's entire plan by separating all the males from the females three months after arriving there.

It didn't take long to realize that if I allowed the indiscriminate breeding to continue, we could have an additional 70 lions on the farm in just one year. Lions are not only sold for hunting but also for their bones. Females are primarily sold for bones because they are not as desired for hunting. Lioness skins are often used as mats or rugs. Males become trophies. They sell the females for R30,000, whereas they may be reimbursed R150,000 to R170,000 for the males.

Many are told that lions are bred to replenish the wild lion population, but nothing could be farther from the truth. The animals are not genetically pure and are bred rapidly, which is not the story told to the public. I have researched this, and there is no validity to the claim that South African wild lions need to be supplemented by captive-bred lions. The South African government will not allow captive lions to be released into wild populations, and the wild spaces are already fully stocked with lions. This is simply a cover story.

The cubs are also sold or rented out to tourist places to be touched and handled, bringing in money to the tourist facility while removing the cost of raising the cubs from the farmer. They come back when they are too big for tourists to play with anymore. When they return, they are sold for hunting, bones, and breeding. Another market is that lions are exported to become pets.

What people who buy cubs don't realize is how sharp their teeth and claws are. By the time they are three months old, they are hard to handle, and at six months, they can seriously hurt people. These people use tools to control the lions—chains, collars, whips, tasers, etc.—to intimidate them. Once they realize how hard big cats are to interact with, many are just left to languish in small cages without getting their nutritional and other needs met. They suffer terribly.

We continued to go back and forth to the farm, but I didn't realize that I was going to end up living there. In early December 2011, I walked around for days asking for a sign. It was a difficult decision because my entire life was back in the Cape. Early in the morning of December 10th, I went for a walk to be at the mountain at sunrise.

As I was walking back, Elias rushed up to me and told me there had been a fight. My friend's father, who had come back from the hospital briefly, had opened the gate and let a lion in with a pregnant lioness, Shanti. A huge fight ensued, and the lion nicked Shanti's jugular vein—she was bleeding out. She had given premature birth to one little cub.

I ran to the fence. Elias had entered the lion enclosure, and my eldest daughter, Taiga, was on the outside of the fence in her pajamas. We watched as Shanti stood up and gave birth to a second cub, which was still enclosed in the umbilical sac. Then she collapsed.

Nancy, an androgynous lion, walked over, pulled the umbilical cord, birthing the placenta, which she proceeded to eat, dragging it and the cub in the membranous sac with her as she walked away. Elias shouted at Nancy, who, luckily, had bitten off enough placenta that she ran off, leaving the cub behind. Elias grabbed the umbilical cord and handed it—and the attached cub in the sack—to me.

I was completely reluctant to become involved by taking this from him. My attitude was that I had no place or right to become involved with lions and lion births. My daughter, Taiga, shouted, "Mom, you have been walking around for days saying you need a sign. This is your sign!"

I said, "I don't know anything about lions!"

She replied, "Mom! You deliver human babies. What would you do if this was a human?"

I said, "First of all, we have got to get her out of that sack immediately."

She responded, "So do it!"

So I took the cord and the dangling sack Elias was handing through the fence, nipped the sack with my teeth, and pulled out the little white cub. She was later named Sienna. I suctioned her a little bit, and as I was doing so, Elias passed the other white cub, who had been sniffling around on the ground this whole time, to Taiga, who put her in her shirt at my instruction.

We walked back to the house, and I called eight different specialists, trying to figure out what to do. I listened to the one who made the most sense and got the specific formula that was recommended. I sent my mother out to drive three hours to Johannesburg to get the correct formula.

That first night with those preemies—two absolutely tiny white babies—feeding and nursing them was one of the longest nights of my life. As I got one to sleep, the other started to scream. It was continuous, and I sat the entire night with these teeny cubs, trying to keep them alive.

I realized that everything in my life had led me to this point. Had I not been a childbirth educator and doula, had I not studied homeopathy or attended so many human births, I would not have known how to deliver Sienna.

Early the next morning, Elias came running back to me and reported that five new cubs were being born to two tawny lions on the other side of the farm. I rushed off to their enclosure, where I watched Clyde kill two little cubs. We saved the three cubs that had survived after the parents moved into the enclosure next door.

Elias suggested we name them after my children. My children were not wild about this idea, so we decided to use our initials and add an "s" for the fifth cub. The two teeny white cubs were named Sienna and Tindra, and the tawny cubs were named Aslan, Reign, and Shannon. This was the birth of the STARS. It changed my life and the life of my children.

I raised a total of 18 cubs in the next three months from birth to survival. All my skills and experience came to good use on the farm even things like practicing karate seven hours a week and being proficient with carpentry and power tools. Everything in my life had led me to this.

When I had been there for three months, I separated the males and females because I saw what the breeding was doing. If we continued, we would have 70 new lions that year. Before conducting my research and interviewing scientists and researchers in the field, I still believed the story that the reason the farm existed was to breed purebred lions to replenish wild populations being decimated by tuberculosis.

So, two years after separating males from females, I thought if every two years we allowed two females to breed and have a few cubs, we'd be controlling the numbers but still doing our duty to conservation. I put two males and two females together in 2013, and Angel of Fire had six cubs in October that year.

Females only have four teats, and it becomes survival of the fittest when there are six cubs fighting for those teats. Typically, three out of six and at most four cubs will survive. Thulani and I watched the six cubs every day. The first four cubs would come to suckle, but when the fifth arrived, Angel of Fire would shake them all off and move 10 or 20 meters away. The cubs, who still had their eyes closed at that point, would worm their way over to her to nurse. The first four would get a drink while the last two slowly grew weaker.

For the first few days, it looked as if every cub was getting a fair chance, but after three days, one of the cubs was getting weaker and weaker. On the seventh day, they died. On day ten, the last cub was not able to reach her. The only time he got close, she swatted him away. That was Taai not getting any milk.

Thulani, who ran everything there and was a true lion whisperer if ever there was one, asked me what I was going to do. At that point, I had already raised 18 cubs and did not want to hand-raise any more. I told Thulani we'd leave the cub to die naturally. Thulani was horrified and exclaimed that we were there to keep lions alive. His response was so honest and true that I decided to pick the dying cub up. We drove into the enclosure and picked up Taai. He lived with me for the first two years of his life.

My boyfriend paid to renovate the ex-taxidermy workshop into a cottage for Taai, my dog Micah, and me across the lawn from my children's cottage. He remained by my side. "Taai" is an Afrikaans word that means something that sticks and you can't get the stickiness off. He was stuck to me and didn't like other people, so he hid if others came around. Taai was my heart.

Over the years at that farm, I saw several examples of the lions knowing something that they had no way of knowing. For instance, in 2015, when the father and my friend were coming back to the farm, they left her house in the Cape at six a.m. All the lions 14 hours away in the Free State began roaring and growling at exactly six a.m. Two of the lionesses broke the electric fence and were trying to escape the enclosure. They did not arrive until 8 p.m., but the lions knew 14 hours before, as they were leaving.

The staff informed me that they always knew when I was coming back from town because Taai, my heart lion, would go to the gate and lie down. He positioned himself at the gate when I was still 20 minutes away.

When I left in 2015, it was under very acrimonious circumstances. My friend and her father had returned and were putting lions back together to breed. They immediately put 16 of the lions up for sale. I was determined to stop them and felt that I had at least 50% claim on the lions. That had been the deal when I stayed to save the place. I successfully stopped five auctions from happening while I was there.

I had lived under never-abating, incredible stress battling to save the place and the cats from auction. My friend and her father couldn't pay me; I did it on my own accord. I was offered, and repeatedly led to believe, that as recompense I was 50/50 owner with them on the whole thing. So, in 2015, when they returned to sell lions, I thought I could stop them.

The reason they came back was that a friend of mine had made a program about what I was doing called *The Lion Queen*. Once *The Lion Queen* aired and millions of people were watching it, my friend and her father decided they wanted to be part of it and came back. Suddenly, after four years of having left me alone without any involvement, they returned.

I told them they could not sell the lions. They told me I had no power. I replied that I did and that I was going to veto this.

It was a huge fight, and my children and I were locked out without so much as a toothbrush. It took several months and a court order for our possessions to be returned to us. They also took my dog, Micah. The day I came to get my possessions, Micah was in the father's truck. He went ballistic, clambering onto the father's lap until he finally let Micah out the door.

I left the farm with two-week-old Mela in a sling, a broken elbow, arm, right hand, and a fractured face with broken cheeks. I left heartbroken.

I started a sanctuary because I needed to care for Mela and get Taai out. Every single day, I looked across at the mountain and told Taai I would not leave him behind. Without these lions to care for, I am not sure I would have scraped myself up and been able to build a sanctuary but because of them, I did.

It is a contradiction, I know. I was so broken I could hardly continue, yet at the same time, I could never un-know what I had learned about lions and the industry. I could never walk away and live an ordinary life without being haunted every minute by what was happening to lions. I am only one person, so I can only do a small amount but even if I only changed a few lives, I had to do it. A driving force behind that was Taai. I couldn't leave him behind once I saw his photo on the 2016 sales catalogue from that farm.

It took several court orders and two years to get some of my lions out. Out of the eighteen lions I had raised like my own children, and dozens I had cared for with love over four years, I was only able to rescue seven.

Of the five STARS, I was only allowed to be reunited with three: Shannon, Reign, and Sienna. I never saw Aslan and Tindra again. In the court settlement, I was offered money, but I chose not to accept funds because I wanted the lions.

I had tried to transform that farm into a sanctuary by creating the Love Lions Alive Project, and had already taken in five lions to sanctuary. So, three of the seven lions I ultimately received included Emma, Amber, and Beau lions to whom Love Lions Alive had already promised lifetime sanctuary. I could not leave them in order to take three of my own much-loved "children" lions.

The other lions I received in the settlement were Taai and Mela. Mela was a two-week-old cub who was with me because her parents, Beau and Ariel, were already mine. However, she was still added to the list of lions that my ex-friend and her father were "giving" to me, even though she was already mine.

That farm had been a breeding facility since its origin in 2002, but under South African law, they are now allowed to convert into a sanctuary. Due to recent legal changes, they will be shut down unless they opt for a voluntary exit allowing them to become a sanctuary. I understand that they have submitted an application to do so.

If approved, they will no longer be allowed to buy or sell lions, allow tourists to visit for exhibition purposes, or bait lions to climb on a Perspex box for photo opportunities. Unlike legitimate sanctuaries in South Africa that rescue lions rather than breed them, that farm has acquired all their lions through breeding or purchase. Still, if they cease the practice of selling lions, I am willing to call them a sanctuary moving forward.

What People Should Understand About Lions

From my personal perspective, lions are magnificently powerful and superior in many ways. They are absolutely incredible. Whenever I am near a lion, beyond their physical power and strength, I am in awe of them energetically and spiritually. I feel privileged. They are superior to almost any other physical being.

To think that anyone has the audacity to treat them as inferior is horrifying. In many zoos, keepers use tasers and shocks just to get them to move so their cages can be cleaned. Those lions could take a person down with one sweep of their paw, but they've been so intimidated that they no longer realize they have that power. They've been broken. Even so, lions recuperate quickly and return to themselves and their power readily.

Just thinking that any human has the right to do that is sickening. Lions are expert thinkers and possess knowledge beyond human understanding. They knew when my grandmother passed away. They walked up to me and rubbed against me, and later my brother called to let me know she had died.

Several cubs have worked together to figure out how to open gates and let each other out. They plan and coordinate.

The messages you share from the cats confirm what I have believed. It helps me when you check in with the cats and share what they say. I wasn't a believer at first. The first time I understood your communication was with the tigers. Something was going on with Igor, and about an hour later I got a call from his former caretakers who were on their way to visit. I had told you Igor wasn't himself, and you told me he was upset because someone was coming. There was no way you could have known and Igor knew they were coming before we did. That was the moment I realized this was real.

I always feel guilt when I leave the lions, but I've learned that I can communicate and connect with them wherever I am. That's helped immensely. I've also learned that those I've lost can still be near me. Instead of feeling bereft, I now feel their energy with me. I am closer to them than ever.

My wish is that people do not diminish lions or see them as victims. Rather, they should hold a vision of them in their minds as powerful and completely in control. Lions are made perfect. Their blueprint is perfection. Every molecule is absolute perfection. If we hold this in our minds, they can return to that state.

Instead of dwelling on how bad things are, we must believe that all is as it should be and that lions will return to their full power. We need to resonate with the belief that lions are amazing, powerful, grand, regal, spiritual beings and see them that way.

Don't reduce them to something that needs to be "saved." I look at them that way from the first moment I meet them. I say, "Let me give you the space and opportunity to return to your full state of lion-ness."

I do not believe I am their rescuer. They are powerful. They are whole. I simply give them the space to be and trust they will return to who they are.

(See Umbahli's interview as an example.)

David and Ansa's Story

While we were greatly inspired by Andi and her work, the primary source of our inspiration was Gareth Patterson[8]. I'm not

---

[8] Well known for his work on the African lion, Gareth Patterson is an environmentalist, independent wildlife researcher and author who has worked tirelessly for more than twenty-five years for the greater protection of African wildlife. Patterson's love for the wild has spurred various projects surrounding animal rights and he has written a number

embarrassed to say that he became a true hero and someone we admire tremendously. Having met him personally and spent quite a bit of time in his company, sharing our love for lions and elephants (the two animals he has dedicated his entire life to), only enhanced our opinion and respect for him.

We have always been deeply invested in animal welfare and have had a soft spot for animals. We were living on the Eastern Cape when we started to become aware of what was going on in South Africa the breeding of lions for the canned hunting industry and for the bone trade. The more we started researching and reading about it, the more horrified we became. This was during the time of the COVID pandemic, and we had a lot of time to process it at home with our domestic cats.

We spent a few days with Andi (from Love Lions Alive/LLA) and had tremendous respect for the commitment she had made to try and rescue these animals. From there, we started supporting LLA and decided we wanted to set up our own sanctuary because there seemed to be more of a need for it.

We were on the doorstep of a natural park, which was one of the most amazing places to go and see elephants in the wild. We loved elephants as our second-favorite animal, but we were always crazy about lions. When we got to see a lion, that would make our day.

---

of fascinating books on the subject. Cathy and I have been inspired by his work as well.

Some people prefer dogs we love cats, and it's a natural progression that we love big cats as well.

This all stemmed from our love of the wild and believing that's where the big cats should be. As a sanctuary, we are trying to fix a wrong. None of these cats should ever be in an enclosure, no matter how beautiful and natural it may be. Humankind needs to start having more respect for wild animals. We see them as sentient beings. We understand that they are free beings and have emotions. It may be difficult for some to accept or understand, but we truly believe in that. We speak to people with that as the foundation the same way you don't go around shooting your neighbors or an elderly parent, people should respect animals in exactly the same way they respect one another.

Once you are physically standing next to an enclosure and you see that lion or tiger, it's almost like you just have to be with them. You realize how amazing they are and how very, very special they are. I feel that if you are in their presence, you understand how magnificent they are, and you feel this deep need. They are so badly exploited, and there are very few ethical sanctuaries in South Africa. You really care and understand their need.

Today we saw Brave at the fenceline, looking at the waterbucks. Then he disappeared into the tall grass, and I said to Dave, "It is so exciting for him to be like that, that we were able to give him that kind of life. He doesn't need people. He doesn't want to see people." We see him every afternoon when we feed him, and he has a little ritual of greeting us when we bring his food. It is just so awesome to see them going back to what they were supposed to be. It's so lovely to see them like that to be that wild animal. There is something magical about these big cats, and you can't not love them and want to be involved.

Everyone has their preferences, and we have always been cat lovers. We love all animals, but we just feel we have a natural affinity toward cats, and we started off with domestic cats. We have twelve of our own.

Differences Between the Big Cats

As Africans, we have grown up around nature and have been taken to nature reserves. We have had quite a bit of exposure to lions, but not to tigers unless you've gone to a zoo or circus. Our initial focus was on lions, but we started rescuing tigers as well. Both are apex predators, but in our experience, tigers have a fantastic array of vocal communications. They are very, very vocal.

Lions also have a unique way of communicating through vocalizations, but they are not as expressive as the tigers. When you are looking at a tiger in front of you, you are in complete awe of the absolutely stunning beauty of this animal you almost have to pinch yourself. It's unreal beauty. They are softer, more expressive, and their eyes are not as piercing as a lion's.

A lion is obviously a majestic-looking animal as well, but a lion has an aura of arrogance of "I don't care about anybody. I am the king of the jungle." So when you are with lions and experience their true aura, when they look at you, you can feel their eyes going through you. With a tiger, they are softer.

With lions in particular, they are very social. Other cats tend to be more independent and seem to prefer being on their own. The dynamics in a lion pride are such that the mother, grandmother, and others will live together for the rest of their lives. The roles they play are important. Then there are the young males who are kicked out of the pride and have to find their own territory, becoming nomadic for a few years.

One of the things we enjoy about the lions here is their social interactions. In a sanctuary, you can't completely replicate the conditions of the wild. Tigers, who would be naturally independent, actually enjoy the company of others in a sanctuary setting. With lions, they are naturally social, even in the wild.

If a trophy hunter shoots the dominant male lion, the result is a power vacuum. Other males will come in and take over that pride, and to preserve their own genetic line, the first thing they do is kill the existing cubs. So if you shoot a male lion, you could end up causing the deaths of another ten to twelve lions.

So many people don't know these things. We had to learn this as well. As the average person, you don't know the family structures or the harm that is done by taking out one lion or one elephant. People must be aware of how these things work in nature.

All the cats have completely different personalities. You get someone like Sem, who is a very gentle lion, and someone like Atlarela, who is a very powerful, quite aggressive lion. He will storm at the fence if you try to take a picture. With lions, you just feel like staring at them and sensing their power and aura. With tigers, they entertain us. The lions are very quiet, and we just observe. It's a fantastic experience just to walk along the fence with a tiger.

Our tigers seem to enjoy seeing us happy. If they do something and notice it makes us happy, they often do it again especially Yehudah. Peter Caldwell, the premier lion vet in South Africa, met him and thinks he's the most relaxed, chilled cat he has ever met. He was chatting. He is so happy, so excited about everything, and nothing gets him down.

Then there's Asmir so serious and so quiet. He is serious, yet so happy to be here. Once he finds his spot for the day, he suns himself and is not likely to move a great deal.

Leila likes to take us for a walk every morning, running behind bushes and jumping up. They are more entertaining, more talkative.

Bina has this new thing where she hides behind a bush to watch Simba and Nala. She jumps at them and charges the fence. She is a mother figure, teaching these two youngsters. With the tigers, we walk with them and talk with them, so it is quite entertaining.

Leopards in the wild are the most elusive of the big cats, and people always say that if you see a leopard, it wants you to see it. If you go to Kruger National Park, you will find them lying up in the big trees and sleeping. Generally, they tend to be more nocturnal, but they are elusive.

Brave is in the bush five or ten inches away, and you'll hear him snarling and growling. Lions do not do this. You can stand there for a couple of minutes and hear where the snarling and growling are coming from, but you cannot see him. Only when he is ready, he suddenly appears like a ghost.

I have been studying the bush for the last ten minutes and have not seen him, yet suddenly he is there. There were waterbuck running against the back of the enclosure, and that made us look up there. Suddenly, we saw Brave.

We can count on one hand the number of times we've seen Brave out in the open. He hides in the bushes, and with all his spots, he is even more camouflaged. Leopards are significantly smaller probably one third the weight of lions and tigers so they can hide easily. Because they are so good at climbing trees, all of a sudden, you will see him lying in one.

It is a fantastic experience to see the different personalities. He is really relaxed. He walks past the vehicle to get his food. We get back into it when the guard serves his food. He walks into his night house, looks at us, and growls a bit. Then he licks his paws and lips and rolls over like a domestic cat. He's showing us that he is relaxed, ready, and trusts us. But it is just not his nature to come running out of the bushes to say hello, like the tigers or lions would do and we don't expect him to ever do that.

We allow him to be as he is. He is showing us his true nature what a leopard is supposed to be. When he is snarling and growling, he is not threatening; it is just the way he communicates. He shows us his beautiful white belly, and his eyes are not aggressive.

When I try to take a picture of him, he charges the fence. I don't like that because I don't want to make him uncomfortable. With the lions and tigers, it's easy to take photos. They are out in the open and out on their decks. His enclosure is very dense and more suited to his natural habitat, so you have to be quick. We don't like to disturb him, but it is important to be able to photograph him.

It has been interesting to discover, through you and Cathy, what an interesting, deep-thinking being he is. He feels like an old soul who has discovered many things and is a spokesperson for the big cats. We'll go and sit under a tree in the shade and chat quietly so he knows we are there and gets used to our voices. But there is no expectation of him walking out to say good morning. We can be there for an hour, and then off he goes. You can feel him watching us. That's what leopards do and we respect that. Whatever we can learn from him is awesome.

When we moved here, there were only a handful of wild leopards in the mountains. But 100 years ago, this was a leopard stronghold. The last wild lion was shot here 150 or 175 years ago, so they did roam this area. There are many streams and other places named after them.

Leopards still exist here, so to have a leopard on the property brings a different dynamic to the area because this is where leopards have been for hundreds of years. The dream one day is to look up in the mountains and see a leopard. There is a chance.

The moment we heard about Brave, we immediately said we would like to offer him a home here. We hadn't been here long when the placing agency came to visit us. When he saw the land and discovered what it meant to us to have Brave here, it made a big difference. He agreed this was the perfect place. And we kind of spiritually connected with Brave from the first moment. He is just so special.

David and Ansa on How to Help

We are saying that people should not support sanctuaries that are not ethical. You need to do your research. Many people are unaware of the negative impact on the animals. When they visit these places, they are amusing themselves at the expense of the animals.

We took our daughters to the circus and zoo when they were younger, but we explained to them that, based on what we know now, it's not right to do that. People need to research before they go, to ensure the place they are visiting is ethical and that the profits are not based on activities that harm the animals. Your money should be focused on the animals' welfare, not on profiting the facility. The more people support ethical sanctuaries, the more sustainable they will be.

We understand this from the perspective of human nature. A lion cub is a very cute little thing. There are people who will pay a lot of money to have their children sit and bottle-feed a lion cub. It's so easy to convince an average person to do this. Many don't want to hear what is actually best for a lion's life. A cub should be sleeping 20 hours a day, but here they are being kept awake for 20 hours a day so humans can have them sit on their laps.

There are many pseudo-sanctuaries that are open to the public. They have restaurants, bars, and cubs, and they make a great deal of money. From our perspective, as an ethical sanctuary, we really have to convince the public not to support those places. You may pay a couple hundred thousand rand it would be far better to take that money and support an ethical sanctuary that is doing something to improve the lives of previously exploited big cats. These places are worse than zoos because of the human interaction, which is not good for the animals. And the animals don't want that.

This all stemmed from our love of the wild and our belief that's where big cats should be. As a sanctuary, we are trying to fix a wrong. None of these cats should ever be in an enclosure, no matter how beautiful or natural it is. Humankind needs to start having more respect for wild animals. We see them as sentient beings. We understand that they are free beings and that they have emotions. It may be difficult for some to accept or understand, but we strongly believe in that. We speak to people with that as our foundation.

In the same way you don't go around shooting your neighbors or an elderly parent, people should respect animals in exactly the same way they respect other human beings.

We made a full commitment to veganism. While some vegans are vegan for health reasons, we do it based on animal welfare grounds. If more people would adopt a plant-based diet, there would be more opportunity to rebuild natural habitats for wild animals to thrive.

There are fewer than 20,000 lions in the wild and fewer than 6,000 tigers. When you compare that to the human population, the ratio is absurd. More people means more cattle, and that means less habitat for wild animals. From a sanctuary point of view, there is no way to soften this it is an astronomically expensive prospect to run a sanctuary. It takes a lot of money to care for these animals, and there is not a lot of focus on financial support for them. We would like people to understand that and consider donating to an ethical sanctuary.

There are very few ethical sanctuaries in South Africa. There are many places where you can pay to walk with or feed lions, and that is completely unacceptable.

Returning to the sacred nature of animals if you have two domestic cats, you will see that they each have very different personalities. They are all beautiful. We have 12 cats, and every single one is different. The same applies to big cats. People don't spend enough time understanding that about wild animals. They have their own personality traits. We really need to start accepting and understanding how important it is to respect these animals for who they are.

Because of the terrible conditions that domestic farm animals live in, we don't believe there is such a thing as a humane death. If you really think about it, not many people are truly connected to this issue, because their meat comes from the supermarket shelf. When you open your eyes, read about it, and understand what is going on, you would honestly be horrified.

It's about looking through the eyes of the animals. The moment you do that, you see feelings, emotions, and a sense of humanity. When you really start to see them, you can't abuse or exploit them because you see them as individuals a living soul.

We spend a lot of time observing elephants. You see the family structure, you see the matriarch leading the whole herd. This is more than just a group of elephants. It's a family.

It's the same with all these animals. When there is a pride of animals, there is a family happening there like Bina, trying to mother Simba and Nala through the fence. It's amazing. When you start looking at animals as individuals, as beings, you can't go back. You have to start trying to make a difference.

Conclusion

The world is evolving. The healers of the Earth understand that we are moving into a higher level of consciousness than ever experienced on the planet before. This shift from our current third-dimensional to fifth-dimensional reality is not a physical shift; it is totally and completely a shift in consciousness.

While the world seems to be falling apart at this time, the chaos we are experiencing is based on our old ways of thinking and being in the world. This shift in consciousness will include heightened awareness and enhanced intuitive capabilities among the people of the Earth, a greater focus on love and our oneness as a species, as well as our oneness with all the beings of the Earth. Lack, limitation, and operating via competition instead of collaboration are on the way out. Love and compassion will prevail.

The big cats and all other non-human beings have operated from a fifth-dimensional reality since their inception on the planet. They have much to teach us. Their messages are powerful and life-changing. An open heart and a desire to respect, connect, and be at peace with all life is the only true path to joy.

I can guarantee you that if you take the cat's advice to heart and step out in practicing some of their suggestions, your life and heart will heal as mine has.